# THE POWER OF CONTENTMENT

## SIRSHREE

Attaining freedom from incompleteness

# THE POWER OF CONTENTMENT
Attaining Freedom from Incompleteness

By **Sirshree** Tejparkhi

Copyright © Tejgyan Global Foundation
All Rights Reserved 2024

Tejgyan Global Foundation is a charitable organization
with its headquarters in Pune, India.

ISBN : 978-93-90132-53-9

Published by WOW Publishings Pvt. Ltd., India

First edition published in July 2024

Printed and bound by Trinity Academy For Corporate Training Ltd, Pune

This book is the translation of the Hindi book titled,
*Santushti* by Sirshree Tejparkhi

---

Copyright and publishing rights are vested exclusively with WOW Publishings Pvt. Ltd. This book is sold subject to the condition that it shall not by way of trade or otherwise, be lent, resold, hired out, or otherwise circulated without the publisher's prior written consent in any form of binding or cover other than that in which it is published and without a similar condition including this condition being imposed on the subsequent purchaser and without limiting the rights under copyright reserved above, no part of this publication may be reproduced, stored in or introduced into a retrieval system, or transmitted, in any form, or by any means, electronic, mechanical, photocopying, recording or otherwise, without the prior written permission of both the copyright owner and the above-mentioned publisher of this book. Any person who does any unauthorized act in relation to this publication may be liable to criminal prosecution and civil claims for damages.

Although the author and publisher have made every effort to ensure accuracy of content in this book, they hereby disclaim any liability to any party for any loss, damage, or disruption caused by errors or omissions, resulting from negligence, accident, or any other cause. Readers are advised to take full responsibility to exercise discretion in understanding and applying the content of this book.

*To the wave that has realized
that it is not a wave but the ocean itself.
The harmony that arises in the wave
with this realization is called contentment.*

# CONTENTS

Introduction     7

Preface     11

## PART I – THE CAUSES OF DISCONTENTMENT

1. Contentment is not Satiation     19
2. The Secret of Discontentment     23
3. Where Does Discontentment Reside?     29
4. The Root Cause of Discontentment     34
5. The Effect of the Body-Mind's Disposition     39
6. Vices that Breed Discontentment – 1     44
7. Vices that Breed Discontentment – 2     50
8. Obstacles in Contentment – Our Internal Layers     56
9. Auspicious Discontentment     62
10. Feel Contented by Making Others Contented     69

# PART II – UNDERSTANDING TRUE CONTENTMENT

11. The Magical Feeling of Havingness — 76
12. All Our Needs Are Being Fulfilled — 82
13. Finding Contentment Through Forgiveness — 87
14. Choosing Contentment in Adversity — 91
15. Finding Contentment Through Patience — 96
16. The Address of Contentment — 102
17. When the Mind and Work Are Not in Tandem — 107
18. The Feeling of Completeness — 113
19. Contentment at Work — 118
20. Towards Supreme Contentment — 124
21. The Perspective for Contentment — 130
22. Principles for Complete Contentment — 133
    Appendix — 139

# Introduction

## The Secret of Contentment

Once, there was a wealthy businessman who had amassed enough riches to sustain his family for seven generations. Despite this abundance, he remained dissatisfied, convinced that just a bit more wealth would finally bring him peace. So, he relentlessly pursued more wealth, yet he never felt contented.

He sought counsel from holy men to find peace and contentment. After searching far and wide, he found a sadhu sitting beneath a tree at a foothill. Bowing respectfully, he said, "Maharaj, I lack nothing materially and am blessed with enough wealth to secure seven generations of my family. Yet, I am plagued by inner discontent, robbing me of sleep. Please guide me toward a solution." The sadhu asked him, "Please tell me the cause of your discontent, and I will give you a solution."

The businessman responded, "I've heard that a person's name is remembered for eight generations. I've amassed enough wealth to support seven generations, but I feel compelled to secure the eighth generation as well. This concern for the future of my family's eighth generation keeps me sleepless at night."

The sadhu smiled, "Don't worry, I will give you a solution. But first, I want you to run an errand for me. There is an old woman who resides in a hut on that hill. Please go and give her this bag of rice. In the meantime, I will find a solution to your problem."

The businessman took the bag of rice and left for the old woman's hut. The hut where she resided did not have a door. The old woman was singing hymns in the praise of God and seemed deeply immersed in bliss.

The businessman kept the bag of rice near the cooking corner and said, "Maa-ji, the Sadhu Maharaj, who resides at the foothill, has sent you this bag of rice."

The old woman replied, "Son, please go and give this bag of rice to some needy person; I don't need it. Please thank the Sadhu Maharaj on my behalf and tell him that I still have enough rice for two days by God's grace. Maybe someone else needs this bag of rice today, and it would be more useful to them."

Upon hearing the old woman's reply, the businessman was startled. He asked her, "But after two days, when your stock of rice is over, wouldn't this bag of rice be useful to you?"

The old woman smiled, "Who has seen the future? Why should I worry today about what will happen two days later? God, who has provided me with food till today, will continue to grace me in the future too. So why should I start hoarding food?"

The businessman was jolted by her reply. He returned to the sadhu, left the bag of rice in front of him, and prepared to leave. The sadhu called him back and asked, "Why are you leaving? Don't you want a solution to your problem?"

The businessman turned around and folded his hands, "Maharaj, I received a solution from the old woman; the solution is contentment. The old woman does not have more than two days' worth of rice, yet she is so contented and happy. I have so much, yet I am still unhappy. If a person who hardly possesses anything is not worried about their future and has full faith in divine providence, then why shouldn't I trust God? I will now surrender all my worries to God; He has already graced me with so much. I will lead a contented life and serve others."

Thus, a brief encounter profoundly deepened the businessman's insight and utterly transformed his life, guiding him toward lasting contentment. He embarked on a journey of selfless service, becoming an example for others to embrace a more positive way of living. How did this happen? Let's explore.

The businessman generously distributed his accumulated wealth, reserved for the next seven generations of his family, to aspiring entrepreneurs who aimed to become self-reliant and create job opportunities for others. He recognized that those seeking his assistance were the very representatives of future generations. Hence, he felt compelled to assist them directly rather than postponing help to his descendants in the distant future.

This story may seem small, but its lesson is profound: Without cultivating the habit of contentment, even if we get everything that we can possibly desire, we will still not value anything. Contentment alone is a great treasure. Without it, all the wealth in the world cannot satisfy us.

True and lasting contentment is a saintly quality. This is not about being a saint or hermit who has renounced worldly life. Rather, it refers to those who live ordinary lives yet embody traits like love, compassion, patience, peace, happiness, devotion, and selfless service. A true saint or sadhu understands the secret to permanent happiness and contentment, valuing it deeply in their life.

Few people today prioritize contentment as an essential quality. Instead, many place utmost importance on amassing wealth, property, fame, and achieving personal goals. It is only when people fail to find the expected happiness after reaching their goals that they begin to recognize the importance of true contentment.

Therefore, ask yourself, "Do I wish for a life filled with contentment? Do I wish to eat, sleep, and nurture my relationships peacefully by being fully content?" If the answer is "Yes," this book will be incredibly valuable.

In modern times, there is a misguided belief that "Only discontentment drives us to achieve great things in life. Contented people lack the fire needed for big accomplishments." However, as we have seen from the story of the contented businessman, this is untrue. Those who grasp the real essence of contentment approach their work with joy and enthusiasm, even while being content. This book aims to teach us the art and balance of true contentment.

Up until now, what you have read is just a glimpse of contentment. To experience true contentment, let us delve into this book and free ourselves from worrying about the future by discovering how to lead a successful, joyful, and fulfilling life.

# Preface
## A Divine Blessing

> "O Lord, please grant me enough, so that neither my family nor any who seek our aid go hungry."

Saint Kabir offers this prayer to God, the Divine Source, from whom he could have requested anything. Yet his plea is humble. He asks only for sustenance, sufficient to ensure that neither his family nor the ascetics who visit them go hungry.

Who can offer such a prayer? Only someone who is truly content. For someone free from greed, the satisfaction of fundamental necessities is enough. Conversely, there are many who remain dissatisfied even when blessed with all the luxuries imaginable. Regardless of their possessions, they perpetually harbor a sense of insufficiency.

Saints and spiritual masters have regarded contentment as the greatest wealth. Our ancient scriptures affirm this: "Contentment is the ultimate happiness, the pinnacle of joy." It is the profound sense of fulfillment derived from embracing all that we have been bestowed with, including our bodies, relationships, societal circumstances, and environment, without harboring any complaints or desires for more. It is about finding fulfillment in our present blessings without becoming ensnared by the pursuit of additional possessions.

However, some people view contentment as synonymous with inaction or laziness. They question how progress would continue if everyone were satisfied with their current circumstances. They argue that the absence of contentment fuels advancement, suggesting that progress would stagnate if man were not driven by discontentment. This belief leads to the misconception that a certain level of discontentment or restlessness is necessary to propel further progress in the world.

Understanding the true nature and depth of contentment is crucial to dispel such misconceptions. Contentment does not entail halting progress or abandoning goals. It is not just a fleeting feeling of satisfaction that comes after reaching a milestone. We often mistakenly believe that obtaining something or accomplishing a specific task will bring us contentment. However, when we achieve these goals, the expected sense of fulfillment often eludes us, prompting us to question why our happiness does not meet our expectations.

**True contentment is not merely a feeling that comes after achieving something. It is our inherent nature, a divine virtue.**

Contentment is a divine virtue, like love, joy, peace, compassion, kindness, and forgiveness. These qualities reflect the true essence of human beings, as each person carries within them the divine essence. At our core, we are expressions of the divine, although this essence can be obscured by ego and ignorance.

Divine virtues are not subject to external factors. For example, genuine love does not rely on receiving love in return. Such a condition would be considered attachment or transactional love. Similarly, compassion and forgiveness do not depend on others reciprocating. They are virtues that radiate unconditionally, like the sun's rays shining equally on everyone.

Likewise, contentment is not dependent on comforts, social status, favorable circumstances, or appreciation. It is possible to experience complete contentment at any moment, regardless of external situation.

If we are not contented now, we can never be, as the human tendency is to perceive lack in every situation. This perpetual longing for external gratification hides the true contentment that already exists within us.

The story of Emperor Ashoka is well-known—a man driven by greed for power and prosperity. He waged wars relentlessly to expand his empire, yet his hunger for more remained insatiable. Despite his conquests, he found himself perpetually discontented. However, when he was graced with wisdom, he chose to abandon his ambitions and embrace the divine path, ensuring others also benefited from the Buddha's teachings. It was then that he attained the true wealth of contentment. This story holds a profound lesson: Despite possessing every luxury, Ashoka remained discontented until he began relinquishing these material pursuits. **This underscores that true contentment is not the result of material gain.**

Saint Tulsidas conveys a similar message in his words:

> "Go-dhan, Gaj-dhan, Vaaji-dhan, aur Ratan-dhan khaan,
> Jab aavey Santosh-dhan, sab dhan dhuri samaan."
> which means
> "A mine of wealth: cows, elephants, horses, and jewels,
> all useless as dust when the wealth of contentment is attained."

The above lines mean that people may amass vast material wealth in various forms—cows, elephants, horses, and jewels. But such possessions fail to satisfy their minds, leaving them in a perpetual state of discontentment. However, when people discover the wealth of contentment, all other forms of wealth lose their significance and become as worthless as dust.

Another example of this is found in the Indian epic, the Mahabharata. Confronted by his relatives and loved ones on the battlefield, the Pandava prince Arjuna was overwhelmed by despondency. He contemplated fleeing the battlefield to seek refuge in the forests. He reasoned with Lord Krishna, questioning the righteousness of winning the war if it meant living with the guilt of killing his loved ones. He expressed his inability to find peace ruling a kingdom, plagued by such anguish, suggesting to renounce everything and live as a recluse in the forest instead. He believed this path would offer him peace, free from the guilt of shedding the blood of his loved ones.

It was in this context that Lord Krishna imparted the teachings of the Bhagavad Gita to Arjuna, guiding him to understand his duties and the necessity of engaging in the battle. This wisdom graced Arjuna with a sense of contentment that was independent of whether he fought the war or its outcome. His contentment stemmed from fulfilling his duty with unwavering righteousness and selfless dedication. The fulfillment of duty, irrespective of circumstances, is indeed a divine virtue.

**This also demonstrates that true contentment, which is independent of present circumstances or future outcomes, motivates dynamic and righteous action rather than promoting laziness or inaction.**

The essence of contentment is vividly portrayed in the lives of Lord Rama and Lord Krishna. Lord Rama found contentment both in his princely life of luxury in the palace and during his exile as a recluse in the forest. Whether waging war against Ravana or relinquishing his mortal form in the waters of River Sarayu, his inner peace remained unwavering. Similarly, Lord Krishna maintained contentment, whether battling demons, joyfully playing with the gopis in Gokul, bestowing blessings, or enduring the curse leading to the destruction of his lineage. Their internal tranquility remained constant, reflecting their profound contentment in every circumstance.

A common thread connects all these examples, the source of their contentment—the ultimate wisdom. Whether they were revered saints like Kabir or Tulsidas, illustrious kings like Ashoka, valiant warriors like Arjuna, or ordinary individuals, true contentment arises only through the realization of our divine nature. This understanding unfolds as we experience our innate essence and express its divine qualities. When we grasp the impermanent nature of the material world around us, a natural sense of contentment emerges in all circumstances.

If you are waiting for a particular event to occur in your life that will bring you happiness and contentment, then abandon that false notion now, as it will never materialize.

If you genuinely seek a life brimming with joy and fulfillment, begin right now. There is no need to change external conditions; instead, focus on inner transformation rooted in an understanding of your true nature. Challenge your beliefs and dispel ignorance. Let go of everything that hinders the expression of your innate qualities. By shedding false beliefs, contentment will naturally radiate from within. Regardless of circumstances, you will affirm, "Yes, I am completely content now."

This book will serve as your greatest ally and guide, helping you peel away the layers of false beliefs rooted in ignorance that have obscured true contentment. Let us embark on this journey together, unveiling the secrets of contentment and integrating them into our daily lives.

# PART I

# THE CAUSES OF DISCONTENMENT

# 1
# Contentment is not Satiation

At a New Year party with his friends, a man with a sweet tooth spotted a dessert stall serving Indian sweets. During dinner, he couldn't stop thinking about saving his appetite for having four gulab-jamuns for dessert. Hastily finishing his meal, he rushed to the stall and ended up devouring five gulab-jamuns! With a loud burp, he declared, "Now I'm fully satisfied!"

As he strolled through the dining hall, he noticed another dessert stall offering rasmalai, one of his favorites. Despite already indulging in five gulab-jamuns, he felt unsatisfied, yearning for a taste of rasmalai. Knowing he wouldn't be at ease without it, he decided to treat himself. Despite having eaten all those gulab-jamuns, he managed to enjoy a full plate of rasmalai. After finishing it, he thought to himself, "Now I finally feel content. Not tasting the delicious rasmalai would have left me with regret."

Later, as he walked past yet another stall offering gajar-ka-halwa, he felt a pang of regret. Despite his desire, he was too full to indulge further. His satisfaction quickly turned to discontentment. Despite consuming many of his beloved sweets, he left the party feeling disappointed and unfulfilled.

The story of this man resonates with a common experience many of us face. We often believe that acquiring a particular thing—a sweet treat, a possession, a success—will bring us lasting contentment. When we finally get it, there is a fleeting sense of satisfaction. However, this feeling does not last because our desires are constantly shifting. The cycle repeats as new desires arise, and we chase after them, mistaking temporary satiation for lasting contentment.

Satiation is the state of being gratified when one's physical needs, desires, or cravings are fulfilled. It is the temporary feeling of satisfaction after obtaining something one desires. **Satiation is a trap that gives us a temporary feeling of fullness. It tricks us into believing that we have found contentment.**

**Take a moment to ask yourself, "What do I want in life—temporary satiation or lasting contentment?"** To find lasting contentment, we must begin by observing our ever-changing desires.

Literature, stories, movies, and plays remind us of the fleeting nature of worldly pursuits. Yet, many people get caught in the worldly illusion, developing vices and addictions that mislead them. Eventually, they feel disillusioned. What once gave them pleasure no longer does, yet without it, they feel empty.

Many people try to imitate the lifestyles of celebrities. Instead of seeing our own lives through the lens of social trends and succumbing to peer pressure, we should live mindfully and confidently with our own originality.

To live a more conscious way of life, it is important to understand that contentment is not the same as satiation. Though they may seem similar, they are very different. Let us take a moment to distinguish between them.

The key difference between contentment and satiation is that contentment is a divine quality. Those who nurture divine qualities within can experience true happiness and lasting contentment.

"Contentment" starts with "C" for "Constant," signifying its permanence and ever-present nature within us. "Satiation" starts with "S" for "Short-lived," indicating its temporary nature. Contentment is an enduring state of joy, peace, and fulfillment, while satiation is a fleeting feeling of fullness or satisfaction that fades quickly.

We often chase after our petty desires, feeling restless and dissatisfied. Fulfilling one desire gives us temporary satiation, which we mistake for true contentment. The space in our mind that was occupied by the desire becomes empty, making us feel lighter and peaceful. However, this feeling is short-lived and soon replaced by another desire, continuing the cycle of discontentment. It is only when we understand true contentment and seek it within that we can break out of this cycle.

For example, Amit recently bought the latest smartphone and felt proud to show it off to his friends. This temporary satiation made him feel special.

Two months later, Amit's friend Rohit bought a newer and more expensive phone. Rohit's display of his new phone made Amit feel inferior. So, Amit sold his new phone at a loss and took a loan to buy an even more expensive one than Rohit's.

Amit thought spending money would bring him contentment, but he only felt temporary satiation. He mistook satiation for true contentment, which is why he never truly felt contented despite spending so much.

Their mutual friend, Sumit, was different. Sumit was happy with his phone, which met all his needs. He was indifferent to the new smartphones his friends flaunted. He did not judge his social status based on his smartphone model and only replaced it when really necessary.

---

**Seeking contentment through sensory pleasures is futile, like trying to fill a bottomless cup with water. Our choices should be driven by the discernment of our true needs, not by sensory indulgence or peer pressure.**

---

So, the first step is to understand the difference between satiation and contentment through our direct experience.

The popular English film "Cool Runnings" shares this memorable wisdom: "A gold medal is a wonderful thing. But if you're not enough without it, you'll never be enough with it." In other words, achieving something is great, but if you are not happy before achieving it, you will certainly not be happy even after you achieve it.

**Points for contemplation**

1. In which aspect of your life do you feel discontented?
2. Reflect deeply on why you feel this way.
3. Think about times when you thought fulfilling a certain desire would make you happy. Did fulfilling it still leave you dissatisfied for other reasons?
4. Reflect on desires you haven't fulfilled yet. Would fulfilling them bring lasting contentment or just temporary satiation?
5. What do you wish your children should value—lasting contentment or momentary satiation? If you want them to have a contented life, what kind of life should you lead?

---

**Case study**

Wilson was watching entertainment videos on a popular social media website. He kept viewing one video after another without end. Lost in this indulgence, he neglected his work, falling behind schedule and leaving tasks incomplete. What advice would you offer Wilson now that you have grasped this chapter?

---

# 2
# The Secret of Discontentment

When contemplating contentment, many people mistakenly believe that neither they nor those around them are contented. But this is a misconception. Contentment is a divine quality inherent within us all. While we all have this quality, various reasons may obscure our ability to experience it, making us feel discontented.

Therefore, when we experience discontentment, we should remind ourselves that we all have the latent potential for contentment within us, even if we cannot access it at this moment. We should say, "Contentment exists within me, but I cannot feel it for now." This empowers us to take responsibility for our emotions and refrain from blaming external factors for our discontentment.

Now the question arises: Why do we sometimes fail to experience the contentment that already exists within us? Let us explore this using an example from Vishal's life.

From a young age, Vishal was driven to excel academically. He dreamed of attending one of the country's top engineering institutes and later pursuing a Master's degree in the US. Though he hoped to attend the Mumbai campus near his hometown, the Institute Council decided that he should attend the Kanpur campus in northern India. Despite his achievement of gaining admission to a prestigious institute, he often felt dissatisfied, even though his friends and family held him in high regard. His discontentment stemmed from the feeling of missing the campus of his choice.

Vishal dedicated the next four years of his life to his graduate studies and then pursued his M.S. degree at an American university. He couldn't get into the university of his choice and had to enroll in another, more expensive university. His friends tried to convince him that the university he had joined was equally good, but he disagreed. Once again, he felt he was missing out on the merits he imagined at his preferred university.

After completing his post-graduation, Vishal secured a job at a prestigious company of his choice. This time, he was overjoyed as he now belonged to the elite IT hub in Silicon Valley. However, he soon realized that the work pressure was high and the living conditions near his office were very expensive and not to his liking. Despite achieving his career goal and beginning to excel at the workplace, he continued to feel dissatisfied with his professional life.

After a few years, Vishal poured his efforts into building his own startup. Despite putting in a lot of effort and investment, he was not satisfied with the growth of his company. Although it was growing, it did not meet the trajectory he expected.

As years passed, Vishal's startup became incredibly successful. However, he began to feel that something was missing in his life. He had neglected his personal life and yearned for more work-life balance. Despite efforts to prioritize family time, he still struggled with feelings of inadequacy and dissatisfaction when compared to his peers.

This is not just Vishal's story but a common experience for many young people today. Despite achieving their goals, they often find themselves still searching for lasting contentment.

---

**Man digs the grave of his contentment by alienating himself from his divine nature.**

---

## The sense of lack

Vishal was constantly discontented at various junctures in his life, feeling as though he was missing or lacking something. This sense of lack is the opposite of contentment. It prevents us from recognizing and appreciating the good and positive things we already have, causing us to focus instead on what we have yet to achieve.

This is similar to a situation when someone is admitted to a hospital, and every family member, relative, and acquaintance comes to visit. However, their focus remains on that one neighbor who has not yet visited.

Many people have such a nature. If they are allowed to capture the present moment within a photo frame, instead of appreciating its beauty and uniqueness, they would say, "This is missing" or "That is lacking."

In the winter, they would say, "It's too cold. If only it were a bit sunnier, things would be better." During the monsoon, they complain, "It's the rainy season, but it's not raining," or "It's been raining all day; when will it stop?" In short, whatever the present moment brings, they always find something missing or lacking.

Those who are habitually dissatisfied often start their day on the same note. For instance, a woman who wakes up early might say, "I am not feeling well. I haven't slept well." She is missing a good night's sleep. If she wakes up late the next day, she might say, "I don't feel fresh," indicating a lack of freshness. In the kitchen, she finds the vegetables she needs are missing. While cooking, she may think, "I'm getting late for work, and no one helps me. No one cares about me." She feels a lack of love. Meanwhile, her father is sitting on the terrace, reading the newspaper and enjoying his retired life. He thinks, "It would be so nice if someone brought me a cup of tea." At that moment, tea is missing in his life.

Interestingly, we often focus on what is missing rather than what we have in our daily lives. We may not even realize that we are constantly chanting the mantra of "missing" in our minds. This subconscious chant has become so ingrained that we are not even aware of it. For instance, when asked about their health, someone with a slight headache might respond, "I have a bad headache," overlooking the fact that the rest of their body is in good health.

Thus, we have become habitual to living in a constant sense of lack. To return to contentment, we must first learn to handle this sense of lack by observing, recognizing, and acknowledging it. The sense of lack is subtle, relating to our deepest feelings, often imperceptible on the surface. It cannot be judged by external appearance or behavior. To dispel this feeling, we must probe it with questions. While we have seen some examples of this earlier, recognizing it within ourselves demands ongoing introspection.

> **Nothing, ever, is missing except your true self. When you are unaware of your alive presence, you feel a sense of lack.**

We must deeply contemplate that the only thing missing is our true self. Understanding that "Nothing is missing except our true self" can be challenging. It implies that we lack recognition and awareness of our true self, which is the constant sense of alive presence.

Rather than focusing on our living presence, we focus on "what is lacking" or "what ought to be." This habit leads us to dwell in the story of the past or imagination of the future, fostering a sense of inadequacy. By embracing the present moment, we can honor everything that constitutes our current reality.

Imagine your relatives visiting you for dinner. After dinner, as everyone chats, you enquire about their well-being, and they reply, "Everything is perfect." Yet, sensing there might be more, you ask specific questions to encourage them to open up. For example, you might enquire, "What else would make this moment even better?" They might respond, "Oh, some frozen dessert like ice cream would be nice." You offer them ice cream and continue, asking, "What else would you like right now?" They might say, "It's hot today. I wish we could have some cool air conditioning."

From the above scenario, you can observe that when you ask your relatives how they are, they initially respond with "All is well." However, as you probe further, you come to realize that they feel the absence of so many things, not just in their lives but also at very moment.

The above example is simple yet profound, and you should also apply it to yourself. Every now and then, ask yourself, "What do I need or desire at this moment?" A variety of responses could emerge, such as, "I'd like something to drink," "I hope my friend calls soon," or "I wish it would rain. It's so hot today."

Ask yourself the above question, particularly when you feel generally satisfied with life and want to see if there is any sense of lack. Assess your comfort with your body, health, emotions, and more. If you still find that everything feels fine, it indicates genuine contentment.

It is important to understand that even when you feel genuinely contented, you may still have ideas about how you can enjoy a better tomorrow. For example, you might think, "Next time, let's order from a restaurant and have a candle-lit dinner at home. We'll invite close friends and arrange for our children to be looked after so we can relax and stay up late. Perhaps we should also have separate conversations for men and women, as their topics often differ!"

If you entertain thoughts like those mentioned above, it signifies that you are content with your current situation but envision ways to enhance your experience of future gatherings with friends. **Right now, everything is fine, but it could be even better in the future.** This mindset acknowledges your acceptance and comfort with the current circumstances and sows the seeds for even greater times ahead. This is the secret to true contentment.

**Points for contemplation**

1. Take two minutes to close your eyes and reflect on what might be missing in your life right now.
2. Consider which aspects of life, such as relationships, career, daily routine, social interactions, health, etc., are causing the strongest sense of lack.
3. Imagine if the cause of this sense of lack were resolved, would you then feel contented? Is there anything else you might still feel lacking?
4. Create a list of things you perceive as missing from your life.

---

### Case study

Anita served dinner to her husband, but instead of focusing on serving, she was preoccupied with how well she had cooked. Even as they ate, she kept asking her husband about the food—whether it was properly cooked, if there was enough salt, etc. She complained about the quality of the vegetables from the market. She felt something was "missing" from the meal she had prepared.

Anita's father-in-law overheard her comments about the food. While he found the food satisfactory, he noticed that Anita made similar remarks daily.

Considering what we have discussed in this chapter, if you were in his shoes, what would you advise her?

# 3
# Where Does Discontentment Reside?

At a wedding reception, guests congratulated the newlyweds. A friend of the groom's mother approached her and said, "Your son has married a wonderful person. She is educated, beautiful, and from a good family." The groom's mother replied, "Yes indeed, by God's grace, everything is perfect, but I wish my daughter-in-law had a sister as well."

Her friend asked, "But she has two brothers, right?" The groom's mother replied, "Yes, she does, but my grandchildren will have no aunt and no one to call 'Aunty.'"

Unfortunately, the human mind often works this way. It finds reasons to feel something is missing, even when there is hardly any chance of complaint!

### Discontentment is just a thought away

Now, the question is, where does discontentment reside? Does it truly exist? Is it real or imaginary? If we ponder these questions, we see that all discontentment resides in the mind in the form of thoughts.

In the example above, the groom's mother had not even considered that her future grandchildren would have no aunt. However, when questioned by her friend, her mind found a reason to feel something was missing. She realized her daughter-in-law had no sister, which triggered the feeling of missing in her mind. She began missing something that wasn't even a present reality but a future possibility!

Unfortunately, many people fall into a pattern of discontentment. They struggle to recognize that this feeling often stems from random thoughts. They might think, "I wish I had more money, felt more energetic, received more love and appreciation, had siblings, or had more recognition on social media," and so on.

People often believe that discontentment is a severe problem, leading them to spend their lives in sorrow and depart the world feeling empty. We must realize that discontentment is merely a thought that can be ended by another thought. As thoughts can cancel each other out, if discontentment is just a thought away, so too is true contentment. We simply need to replace thoughts of discontentment with thoughts of contentment.

### The effect of intense thoughts

Accepting that discontentment is just a thought can be challenging for those who are deeply discontented. They might question how a mere thought can have such a grave impact on their emotions. Indeed, fleeting thoughts usually do not cause much unhappiness. For instance, if we miss a train because we arrived late, we may regret it for a moment, but that feeling soon passes when we catch the next train.

Intense negative thoughts can become so potent and ingrained within us that they get integrated into our belief system. This can result in a lasting sense of discontentment, which may persist even in the afterlife. Ultimately, our belief system is shaped by these deep-rooted thoughts.

The root cause of discontentment lies in these negative, deep-rooted beliefs that prevent us from being happy even when everything is fine. For example, some deep-rooted social beliefs are: Everyone should get married, everyone should marry by a certain age, everyone should have children by a certain age, everyone should have two children, it is necessary to have a male child, a wife must look after the house while the husband works outside to support the family, etc. Many of these social beliefs are so strong that they get ingrained in our DNA! If even one of these social beliefs is not satisfied, someone in society will always remain discontented about it.

Just one false belief can severely affect our lives. Society imposes numerous strict beliefs about how men and women should look and behave, including their skin color, height, appearance, status, personality, skills, and occupation. If someone fails to conform to even one of these beliefs, they will be criticized and treated unfairly.

For example, a wealthy, educated lady had two daughters. However, she was discontented throughout her life because of her belief that a son is necessary to continue her lineage. It would have been much better for her if she had changed this incorrect belief. She could have considered adopting an orphaned boy or believed that both sons and daughters are equal.

A girl suffered depression due to her inferiority complex about her dark skin. A boy committed suicide because his parents compelled him to become an engineer when he wanted to be a designer.

Our incorrect beliefs make not only our lives but also the lives of those around us miserable.

---

**Rather than regretting our mistakes at the end of our lives, it's better to recognize them in time and take corrective action so we can live the rest of our lives in contentment.**

---

Once, a lady attended a satsang and said to the guru, "Guruji, I am happy in every way, but my daughter does not have a child yet. If this were resolved, she would be very happy."

The guru asked everyone at the satsang, "Those who have children, please raise your hands." Half of the attendees raised their hands. The guru then asked, "Now, of those with their hands raised, please keep your hand raised if you do not have any sorrow in your life and are very happy and content." Hearing this, everyone lowered their hands, as despite having children, they still harbored some other incorrect beliefs, keeping them in a state of discontentment.

The guru then told the lady, "Your daughter will not find contentment by having children. She will only experience contentment once she lets go of the incorrect belief that having a child will bring her happiness."

We often harbor many incorrect beliefs that keep us in a perpetual state of discontentment. For example, "More money means more security and happiness," "Without showing anger, no work gets done," "Others should complete everything on time just like I do," "Others should be perfectionists like me," etc.

Whenever we feel discontented in life, we must examine if an incorrect belief is the root cause. If so, removing this incorrect belief is the solution. For instance, having a brighter skin tone is not the solution, but letting go of the belief that "Being dark-skinned is not good" is the right solution. Similarly, expecting everything to go exactly as we wish is not logical. Instead, removing the belief that "Everything should go exactly as I wish" is the right solution.

**Points for contemplatation**

1. If you are discontented about something in your life, identify the specific incorrect belief causing this discontentment. If you are content now but feel discontented in the future, do this self-examination.
2. Are you discontented with your physical health, mental well-being, social life, or financial security?
3. Are you discontented with your family in any way? If yes, then examine in detail the incorrect beliefs underlying this discontentment.
4. Do you or the people around you have any negative traits that dissatisfy or frustrate you, which you would like to

change? Identify the deep-seated incorrect belief causing this discontentment.

5. Once you find these specific incorrect beliefs, start intentionally letting go of them by consistently working on yourself.

---

**Case study**

Neha worked as a project manager in a multinational company. She had developed the pattern of being a perfectionist. One day, she was asked to give a presentation at an important meeting. Her assistant prepared the presentation according to her guidelines. During the presentation, one of the clients pointed out a mistake and corrected Neha.

After the presentation, Neha vented her frustration on her family and skipped dinner. She blamed them, along with her assistant and everyone else, for the mistake in her presentation. The incident left her feeling discontented for days ahead.

One day, Neha meets you at a coffee shop and recounts the entire incident in detail. What would you advise her?

# 4
# The Root Cause of Discontentment

An elderly man named Hiralal lived a peaceful, smooth, and trouble-free life. His wife was kind-hearted and dedicated to serving others. Their children were well-educated, successful, and deeply respectful toward their parents. Hiralal had ample wealth and enjoyed good health.

He had good relations with all his neighbors and was widely respected. People would look at Hiralal and think, "Everyone should live a retired life like him. He's so happy and seems to live in heaven!"

But did anyone ever ask Hiralal if he truly lived in heaven or hell? Every morning, the first thing he did was check the stock market to see if his shares had appreciated. Still in bed, he would read all the negative news of the day, starting each day with a sense of disappointment.

Hiralal also believed that if his first cup of morning tea wasn't perfectly sweetened, his entire day would sour. This habit of sowing seeds of discontentment would set the tone for his day. By evening, those seeds would grow into towering trees of dissatisfaction.

Throughout the day, he would find evidence that reinforced his belief. A chance encounter with someone he disliked on his way to the temple was a sign that his day was doomed. A lunch not to his taste would enrage him. Even during prayer, he would see a breeze extinguishing the temple lamp as a bad omen. He would then call his relatives and children, seeking reassurance of their well-being. If someone parked their vehicle in his parking area, though it stayed empty all day, it irritated him. Thus, Hiralal was disturbed by trivial daily incidents, preventing him from leading a happy and contented life.

What was the reason for this? Were the incidents the actual cause of Hiralal's discontentment? No! The real cause for his daily discontentment was his habit of making mountains out of molehills by exaggerating trivial daily happenings.

**At the least, don't get stuck and distressed over trivial occurrences by giving them undue importance.**

Just like Hiralal, many people lose their peace of mind by giving needless importance to trivial incidents in their daily lives. Others, who observe them externally, often envy them and aspire to lead a happy and successful life like them. But the sad fact is that these people, whom others envy, usually live in sorrow and discontentment, believing they can be contented only when everything is perfect, to their liking. Unfortunately, this never happens.

Once, a demon prayed to God and performed intense penance and *sadhana*. God was pleased with him and asked, "What do you want?" He replied, "I want to rule over all the people in the world. I want to reside in their minds and hearts."

God replied, "This is impossible, but I can grant you this wish: If any person willingly invites you, you can take charge of their minds and hearts."

The name of this demon is Discontentment. He never goes anywhere by himself, but if someone willingly invites him, he settles in their minds and hearts. No big reasons are required to invite him; trivial matters are enough, as he is always ready to reside within anyone's mind and heart.

Consider some examples: You wish to see a movie but don't get tickets. The dress you want to buy is sold to someone else. A new mobile is launched, but it is out of stock by the time you go to purchase it. You order things online, only to find many items are unavailable. You plan to go somewhere but are interrupted by unexpected guests and have to cancel the plan. You go to a restaurant but do not get your favorite corner table. Your favorite team loses the championship final, and their loss stays on your mind, making you feel discontented for weeks. Even the losing team members probably would not be as disappointed.

In the many years of your life, how often have you been caught up in minor daily incidents and lost your peace of mind? When this becomes a habit, remaining in a state of discontentment becomes your second nature. Even a trivial reason can cause you discontentment.

Therefore, stop getting disturbed with minor daily incidents. Break this pattern and develop the habit of living in a state of peace and contentment despite trivial incidents so that you can tackle the major challenges of life more effectively.

---

**A conducive environment and conveniences are necessary to live comfortably in the external world. To be happy, peaceful, and contented, it is essential to either realize our true nature or be in fervent love with God.**

---

## Two mantras for averting discontentment

Often, we find ourselves stuck in two kinds of situations. The first is when a past event stays with us, refusing to fade away. We replay it in our minds, feeling disturbed, regretful, and disappointed. Thoughts like, "I wish I had responded differently," "I wish I hadn't said that," or "I wish things had gone differently" keep us stuck in this loop of regret and discontentment.

Such negative thoughts invite the demon called Discontentment into our minds and hearts. Drive out this demon using the mantra, "Let it go." What is done is done, so release it from your mind. When troubling memories arise, repeat the "Let it go" mantra to regain your peace.

For example, if you miss the bus, let it go. Calmly wait at the bus stop for the next one. If you miss a crucial opportunity, avoid dwelling on it with discontentment. Instead, repeat the "Let it go" mantra to free your mind and patiently await the next opportunity. If the item you wanted to purchase is out of stock, let it go. It will become available again. Life has not come to an end. At least, do not hold onto trivial things. Let them go.

The second scenario is when you find yourself in an ongoing situation that you dislike or feel uncomfortable in. In such cases, use the mantra "Let it be." This means allowing the situation to unfold without resisting it or getting deeply entangled in it. Maintain detachment until the situation is naturally resolved.

For example: If there is too little sugar in your tea or too much salt in the food, it doesn't matter. Repeat the "Let it be" mantra. These are small incidents in the big journey of life! If unwelcome guests visit you, tell yourself, "Let it be. It's not a big deal. This too shall pass." If your boss unjustly shouts at work, tell yourself, "Let it be. No one's words can disrupt my peace." When you are trying to sleep and dogs bark in the neighborhood, say, "Let it be. Every creature has a right to express itself! They'll calm down soon." If children make a mess despite your liking for cleanliness, remember to say, "Let it be. They're just kids."

This way, you can retain your peace of mind during and after minor incidents. This practice will also prevent discontentment from becoming second nature. Make it a daily habit to maintain your peace of mind with these two mantras: "Let it go" and "Let it be."

**Points for contemplation**

1. Are there past incidents that still disturb your peace of mind when you think about them? If yes, release these thoughts using the "Let it go" mantra. Notice if you feel better and more contented after using this mantra for a while.
2. Do you find yourself easily upset by minor incidents?

3. What daily occurrences disturb your peace of mind? For instance, someone might feel unsettled because their child is not wearing shoes properly. Are there such trivial incidents that bother you? If so, try using the "Let it be" mantra and observe any changes over time.

---

**Case study**

In the digital age, social media significantly influences today's generation. Young people enjoy posting photos, always ensuring they present their best selves.

Sakshi used to get deeply upset by negative comments on her photos or posts on social media. Just one comment could ruin her entire day. She also constantly compared herself to others with similar social profiles. Over time, this habit made it hard for Sakshi to forgive herself and others for trivial mistakes and incidents.

In this situation, what would you advise Sakshi?

# 5
# The Effect of the Body-Mind's Disposition

Discontentment is merely a thought, but not all people get the same thoughts. Each one has different thoughts that lead to their discontentment.

Someone might be dissatisfied because their shirt is not as white as someone else's. Another might dislike wearing white shirts altogether but have to wear them. A third person might be discontented because he loves white shirts but has only two. All three are discontented but for different reasons.

Looking deeper, we see that discontentment stems from one's basic disposition, the predominant nature of one's body-mind mechanism. For example, two colleagues might have similar tasks but feel discontented for different reasons.

One colleague is discontented because he feels he is not assigned enough work, hindering his learning and progress. The other feels overwhelmed with too much work. In his previous job, he would finish his work in 3 to 4 hours, but now he has to work for 8 hours. So, while one wants more work, the other wants less.

Thus, the root cause of their discontentment lies in the dispositions of their body and mind, inclinations, and core values. When we hear someone expressing their discontentment, we can understand the actual cause, which is their disposition. Similarly, understanding one's disposition allows us to gauge what can make them discontented.

There are three types of body-mind dispositions: *Satva*, *Rajas*, and *Tamas*. The relative proportion of these attributes determines the nature of one's body-mind. Every person has all three attributes in varying proportion. Some may be predominantly Satvic, others Rajasic, and some may be dominated by Tamas.

The root causes of discontentment vary among people with different predominant dispositions. Let us understand how.

**Causes of discontentment with Satva-dominant people**

Satvic traits include equanimity, balance, virtuousness, forgiveness, kindness, empathy, and fairness. However, Satvic people can also suffer from discontentment.

For instance, someone seeking higher wisdom might feel discontented because they cannot find time to read all the major spiritual literature. Reading one book might make them think they have sacrificed reading another, causing discontentment.

A devotee might feel discontented because other responsibilities prevent them from completing their daily chanting or worship rituals.

Someone who serves others might feel discontented because while serving one, they might see four others who need their service. Their inability to serve everyone makes them discontented.

Someone who meditates may feel discontented because the ideal environment for practice is not available. They might even consider leaving home and family to retire to a forest for uninterrupted meditation.

In this way, Satvic people have their own reasons for feeling discontented and unhappy.

**Causes of discontentment with Rajas-dominant people**

Rajasic individuals exhibit traits like hyperactivity and uncontrolled ambition. They enjoy working hard. If they attain a sense of balance in life, they can discern when to work and when to rest. However, when Rajas dominates their nature, they can become uncontrollably workaholic. They keep moving from one task to the next without a pause. They just cannot stay still and must keep doing something all the time.

People with a Rajasic nature often feel discontented due to a perceived lack of time. They believe they have too much to accomplish in too little time and may even lament over the mere 24 hours in a day!

Being highly ambitious, they relentlessly pursue fame, position, and power. This constant pursuit becomes a significant cause of their discontentment. Once they achieve one goal, they immediately set their sight on the next. They seldom fully enjoy the rewards of their accomplishments because their focus is always on the next goal. While they may briefly experience satisfaction, true contentment eludes them. An excess of Rajas can leave anyone permanently discontented.

**Causes of discontentment with Tamas-dominant people**

Laziness, carelessness, excessive sleep, and daydreaming are traits of those dominated by Tamas. They find many reasons to be discontented. They desire life's comforts without striving for them and expect everything to align with their wishes while making minimal effort themselves. They rely on others to do things for them and seek to earn more with less effort, often resorting to shortcuts to advance in life. A Tamasic person will use any means to complete tasks with minimal exertion, often procrastinating and offering excuses rather than finishing promptly. This tendency can lead them to lie and deceive to justify their standpoint.

Due to their indolence, Tamasic people often face failures but blame others. They also tend to blame their fate. For instance, if they do not exercise out of laziness and overeat, they blame fate for their weight gain or poor health.

### A balance in the three dispositions leads to a contented life

To remove discontentment from your life, you must first identify and clearly understand its hidden cause. If your discontentment stems from your body-mind's predominant nature, you can balance this and achieve contentment.

For example, a Tamasic person will feel discontented when required to exert or complete tasks. They will also face further discontentment from the consequences of missed deadlines. Balancing their Tamas can lead them to experience contentment in life.

However, balancing one's basic nature takes time. This can be achieved through discipline, self-control, adherence to rules, and setting principles, which will be discussed in the following chapters. For now, we are only trying to understand how the nature of our body-mind is the root cause of our discontentment.

Only by accurately identifying the problem can we work toward finding a solution. We need to think deeply about the fundamental nature of our body-mind to understand the root cause of our discontentment. In subsequent chapters, we will also discuss anomalies in human nature that increase discontentment.

### Points for contemplation

1. Considering the three types of human disposition we have explored, reflect on which one is predominant within you.
2. Delve into which type of nature is primarily responsible for your discontentment: Tamas, Rajas, or Satva.

## Case study

You may already know about *Vata*, *Pitta*, and *Kapha*—the presiding tendencies of our body, according to Ayurveda, that influence its physiology. Let us explore a case study that illustrates how specific mental and physical characteristics affect a person.

Isha is Satvic by nature and has a Kapha body type. Her Satva drives her thirst for wisdom, but she frequently catches colds and suffers from sinusitis, making it challenging for her to read spiritual literature. She often laments to others that her frequent cold and painful sinuses have significantly impacted her quality of life.

Asha is inherently Rajasic and has a Vata body type. She is constantly engaged in activities, especially in her kitchen. However, she frequently complains about joint pains that slow her down. Unintentionally, she often voices her frustration about the lack of time in her life to others.

Nisha is predominantly Tamasic and has a Pitta body type. She keeps procrastinating on her tasks and also struggles with hyperacidity and digestive issues.

How would you advise them to recognize their mental and physical dispositions, acknowledge their shortcomings, and balance the inherent nature of their body-mind?

# 6
# Vices that Breed Discontentment – 1

Man can fall victim to the ego. Where ego exists, its offshoots appear as vices such as comparison, greed, anger, attachment, lust, delusion, insecurity, ambition, superiority, inferiority, laziness, hopelessness, and more. These vices breed discontentment, regardless of one's body-mind disposition.

Now, let us explore the fundamental vices that are the root cause of our discontentment.

**Comparison**

Comparison among people is a significant cause of discontentment. For instance, we might be happy with our mobile phones, but seeing a friend or neighbor with the latest smartphone can make us discontented. Similarly, if a neighbor buys a new premium car, we may start feeling unhappy with our own.

Sanjeev was delighted with his life. He had a good job and salary, comfortably providing for his family. One day, he met his childhood friend Saurav. During school, Saurav struggled academically and often copied Sanjeev's answers to pass exams. Sanjeev used to wonder about Saurav's future and who would employ him. However, Saurav had become a successful entrepreneur, owning a large bungalow, a fleet of cars, servants, and many amenities. After meeting Saurav and hearing about his achievements, Sanjeev felt dissatisfied with his life for the first time. His accomplishments seemed insignificant compared to Saurav's, filling him with deep discontentment.

When Leena met her friend Varsha, she observed and assessed Varsha's clothes, jewelry, footwear, and accessories, noting whether the jewelry was made of gold or diamonds. She was also curious about the interior decor and kitchen arrangement at Varsha's house. She started comparing what she observed with her own and felt discontented.

When we visit a garden, we see many different kinds of flowers, all coexisting happily without comparing themselves to each other. Only we, humans, make comparisons and judgments, poisoning our lives with discontentment. We often wonder, "Why don't we have what others have?" and make ourselves perpetually discontented. To lead a happy and contented life, we must let go of the habit of comparison and learn to be satisfied with what we have.

**Greed**

Greed is a vice that hinders true contentment. Nothing is ever enough for someone afflicted by greed; they always want more. This perpetual desire is the root cause of their discontentment.

A Satvic person will always desire more knowledge, more opportunities to render service, and more time for prayer, chanting, and meditation. A Rajasic person will constantly strive to do more work and achieve more. A Tamasic person will desire more rest and sleep and want to gain more by doing the least work.

We might feel that a Satvic person's desires are not greed. After all, seeking knowledge, rendering service, and engaging in prayer and meditation are positive pursuits. However, there should be no discontentment in these activities. If these pursuits lead to discontentment instead of joy, it indicates a lack of proper understanding of their purpose. It means they may still be bound by their desires, and their devotion may lack true surrender.

Whatever positive activities we engage in, such as meditation, prayers, service to others, and acquiring knowledge, must always be accompanied by a sense of joy, not discontentment. This perspective will be elaborated further in subsequent chapters, exploring how Satvic activities can be performed without any trace of discontentment.

People also desire to be the first to do or complete things, or at least to not lag behind others. This is often called performance pressure, where individuals feel compelled to innovate or excel, particularly in the workplace, to outshine colleagues and impress superiors. If pursued with positive intent, this drive can be beneficial. However, this desire can indirectly lead to greed if not managed properly.

> **One can never be satisfied by trying to fulfill sensory cravings. The sooner we gain conviction about this, the earlier we can tread the path of liberation and contentment.**

### Envy

Envy is a vice that prevents anyone from finding contentment in life. It is a consuming fire that people often burn themselves with, yet it never gets extinguished. The consequences of this vice include sorrow, restlessness, discontentment, anger, and even wrongdoings. Envy sometimes even leads to crime, which eventually culminates in regret.

Those who are naturally envious feel discontented by the success and achievements of others. Sadly, people often envy their loved ones—brothers envy brothers, sisters envy sisters. It extends to friends, relatives, family members, and neighbors, frequently causing strained relationships.

Sometimes, it can escalate to the point where people commit crimes. Those consumed by envy may not hesitate to harm others, but this behavior is ultimately self-destructive. Let us understand this with an example.

Rupali and Suhani were two authors who had become good friends over social media. Both used to share their ideas, encouraging and supporting each other in their writing endeavors. Rupali was more talented than Suhani as an author. She started getting better writing projects and won several awards. Due to this, Suhani started becoming envious of Rupali. She couldn't see that Rupali was working harded than her. She felt that Rupali had begun to perform better due to the suggestions and ideas given by her. She started getting annoyed with Rupali's success and began spreading rumors about her, such as, "Rupali copies others' ideas," "Rupali has also been building up her network in an incorrect manner and gaining success unfairly, etc."

Even after all her actions, Suhani still wasn't satisfied. She created fake social media accounts to bully Rupali on all platforms. Eventually, Rupali became fed up with the harassment and reported the case to the cyber-crime department. Upon investigation, Suhani's actions were revealed. This revelation shocked many. Due to her envy, the losses Suhani had to endure far outweighed Rupali's losses. She tarnished her reputation, lost a good friend like Rupali, and her peace of mind. Furthermore, she was labeled as a criminal.

From the above example, we can see that envy is a vice that can destroy us completely. This vice should be identified, acknowledged, and eliminated from the roots of our nature. Anyone who wishes to experience true contentment must stay away from envy permanently.

**Distrust**

Some people find it difficult to trust anyone and feel nothing wrong about it. They believe they are safeguarding themselves by not trusting anyone. They believe that no one in this world is trustworthy and fear they might get hurt if they do. However, they fail to recognize their habit of distrusting people as a vice. Distrust is indeed a vice because it prevents us from leading a carefree, happy, and contented life.

People who struggle to trust others often live in fear. They are constantly suspicious of those around them. As they cannot rely on others, they try to handle everything themselves, leading to a tense and stressful life. Consequently, their loved ones may distance themselves, reinforcing their belief that no one cares, loves, or supports them. These thoughts perpetuate a sense of discontentment in the life of a distrustful person.

It is essential to realize that the world is like a mirror. How we perceive and think about others internally, is reflected in our external experiences. When we begin to trust others internally, this trust can be reciprocated externally. While it is important not to trust everyone naively, we should strive to develop faith and trust in worthy individuals around us and overcome negative beliefs about distrust. This shift can significantly enhance our sense of contentment in life.

**Points for contemplation**

1. Reflect on whether there has been a time in your life when you were contented, but after meeting someone and learning about their life, you began comparing yours with theirs and became discontented.
2. Examine whether your discontentment is caused by another person. Do you feel that everything the other person possesses—material things, talents, skills, and opportunities—should also be available to you?
3. Assess whether you find it easy to trust people. If not, consider why this might be the case. Do you frequently experience discontentment in your relationships?
4. Whether at home or in the workplace, engage in small trust-building exercises to cultivate faith and confidence in others.

**Case study**

In Indian mythology, Ravana is a well-known demonic figure known for his vices, such as arrogance, greed, comparison, and envy. If you could advise him today, how would you show him a mirror reflecting the vices that caused his discontentment? This reflection could help him understand the root causes of his unhappiness.

# 7
# Vices that Breed Discontentment – 2

In this chapter, we will delve into more vices that lead to discontentment.

**Ambition**

"We all need ambition to advance in life" is a true statement, as long as it does not compromise our peace, happiness, and contentment. However, excessive ambition can become a disease, gradually undermining our mental and physical well-being.

People often argue that progress in life is impossible without ambition. However, if people learn to work with a detached enthusiasm, their goals will begin to align with the divine will. Then, they can act without attachment to outcomes. This approach prevents frustration from failures or discontentment and curbs excessive ambition. It also improves the quality of action, as the opportunity to act becomes a reward in itself.

Detached enthusiasm means working with full passion and vigor and focusing on the goals while remaining indifferent to the outcome. Thoughts about the result should not diminish the enthusiasm for the work itself. Those who work with indifferent enthusiasm are rarely troubled by negative results.

People consumed by excessive ambition are never satisfied. They live in perpetual discontentment throughout their lives, always wondering if they have left any work unfinished, even on their deathbed.

Some people realize as they face death that they have spent their entire lives and energy running around aimlessly without achieving anything meaningful. Alexander the Great regretted this in his final hours. He famously instructed that his hands be left open as his body was carried to the grave, symbolizing that despite conquering vast lands, he departed this world empty-handed.

Ambition increases one's drive to work, as does the desire to serve others. However, there is a distinction between these two motivations, which we will understand with a story.

Two young men, Sameer and Deepak, left their village for the city to become engineers. Both shared a desire for their village to have internet facilities, enabling everyone to benefit from modern communication systems. However, for Sameer, this goal was driven by ambition, while Deepak saw it as a service to their village community. Let us explore why this was the case.

Sameer viewed this goal as a business opportunity. He aimed to provide internet services to the village, intending to profit from it. His plan involved making villagers habituated to entertainment like online video games, OTT platforms, and social media, ensuring they couldn't do without internet access.

> **Pursuing goals dictated by popular opinion or fate does not bring contentment. True peace, happiness, and lasting fulfillment come from goals that align with the divine will.**

In contrast, Deepak aimed to provide internet facilities in their village for the welfare and progress of the villagers. He aimed to introduce online education, banking services, and work-from-home opportunities to boost employment locally. Deepak envisioned a brighter future for the village youth, offering online courses and coaching to enhance their prospects.

Thus, Sameer and Deepak had the same goals but different intentions. The underlying intentions always affect the outcome of any goal. If there is a personal agenda or an intent of only satisfying oneself behind the fulfillment of any goal, then this is driven by ambition. An ambitious person will never be truly contented; he will be too busy compounding his profits.

If the underlying intent behind a goal is selfless service, it aligns with the divine will and brings true contentment. In this scenario, the individual works selflessly for others, leaving the outcome to God. This service is performed selflessly with detachment, accepting the results as the divine will.

If we can shift the intention driving any goal from ambition to selfless service, we can experience true contentment. This approach is possible only for those who understand the value of a happy and contented life. However, those who remain unaware, continue to pursue their ambitions, trapped in the rat race of life.

## Superiority and inferiority

Both superiority and inferiority lead to discontentment. A person with a superiority complex always wants to be the center of attention, seeking respect and admiration from everyone. When this does not happen, they start complaining that no one cares about them and vow to show the world their worth one day.

Similarly, a person with an inferiority complex constantly indulges in self-criticism and leads a narrow, closed life. They often blame fate, God, or others for their unhappy life.

Due to a lack of knowledge, people often suffer from superiority or inferiority. However, when they attain wisdom, they realize that no one is superior or inferior, big or small, good or bad. Everyone is the same, as everyone comes from the same Divine Source. Everyone is complete and content within themselves. Any discontentment arises only from incorrect thoughts and beliefs. Once these misconceptions are removed, all unnecessary sorrow disappears, and true contentment reigns supreme.

If someone suffers from an inferiority complex because of their physical appearance, they should read about devout and wise Indian saints like Soordas and Ashtavakra. They reached the pinnacle of spiritual attainment by dedicating their bodies to the ultimate purpose despite physical handicaps. After learning about their journeys, one would realize that no one is superior or inferior; everyone is the same.

**Paying attention to what others say**

Suman was a homemaker who lived very happily with her family. Her husband, a busy businessman, could not devote much time to the household, so Suman took on the responsibility of running the home. She cared for her children and in-laws and sometimes even helped her husband with his work. She also managed activities outside the house. Everyone in the house loved and respected Suman, and she lived a happy life.

One day, Shalini, Suman's childhood friend and a school principal, visited her. She asked Suman, "What do you do all day at home? Don't you get bored?"

Suman replied, "I don't have time to get bored. There is always some work to be done in the house."

Shalini burst into laughter and exclaimed, "That's wonderful! You're living the life of a glorified maid and enjoying it! It saddens me when innocent women like you are deceived in the name of love, especially by those close to you. Hire a couple of servants to manage the household and start exploring outside. Life can be delightful."

After hearing this, Suman was deeply disturbed. She began noticing flaws everywhere despite having everything in life and started feeling dejected. She genuinely began to believe that her family members were taking advantage of her. As a result, her mood worsened, leading to arguments with everyone in her family. The entire family was engulfed in sadness, stress, and discontentment—all because Suman took Shalini's words to heart.

In the Indian epic Ramayana, Queen Kaikeyi also committed this same mistake. She heeded the advice of her maid Manthara and orchestrated Lord Rama's exile for fourteen years so that her son Bharat could become king. This decision caused profound sorrow and turmoil for the entire royal family.

If we observe closely, we will find several characters like Manthara in our daily lives. We must use our discernment to avoid listening to such influences and ensure we do not let them poison our lives with discontentment.

To achieve this, we must respect and recognize the value of our work and be grateful for what we have in life. When we adopt this mindset, we become less susceptible to being disturbed by others' words.

The mind can indeed harbor numerous vices, including over-thinking and anger. We must take responsibility and explore deeply within ourselves to understand the root causes of our discontentment. Once we identify these causes, we can take proactive steps to address and mitigate these issues effectively.

**Points for contemplation**

1. Do you currently have any ambitions or desires that make you feel discontented?
2. If you let go of these ambitions or desires, would you feel more contented?
3. How much attention do you usually pay to others' opinions? Has someone ever said something that made you feel discontented?

**Case study**

In the Indian epic, the Mahabharata, two brave warriors, Arjuna and Karna, stand out. While Arjuna remained contented, Karna kept seeking satiation and validation in a life bereft of royal lineage. Had it been possible, what would you advise each of them?

# 8
# Obstacles in Contentment – Our Internal Layers

Most of the regrets and discontentment we experience are often related to others. We are intricately connected with so many different people through several relationships, like personal, professional, social, family, neighborhood, friends, and foes. These interactions give rise to most of the discontentment.

In fact, the closer the relationship, the greater the level of discontentment. This is because we expect the most from people closest to us and when these expectations are not met, we become sad and discontented.

Some instances of discontentment run so deep that they become wounds, which in turn accumulate within the mind as layers. These wounds make us mentally and physically sick and also affect our decision-making. As a result, we repeatedly make wrong decisions and lead a life devoid of joy.

For example, Shivram's son married his girlfriend against his father's wishes. Out of anger, Shivram asked the newlywed couple to leave his house. Then he kept lamenting for the rest of his life, "My own son has caused me so much grief. I have done so much for him, and this is how he has repaid me. So ungrateful!" Shivram led the rest of his life in sorrow and discontentment.

On the other hand, Shivram's son also remained unhappy and discontented, thinking, "What would have gone wrong had my father just accepted us? This is my life, after all! He could have allowed me to happily make my own choice. But he always imposed his way in everything. He never empathizes with others' feelings."

Imagine how much suffering his girlfriend would have endured if Shivaram's son had married according to his father's preference. It would have formed severe injured memories within her, making her feel rejected and discontented.

In this way, people harbor feelings of disappointment, stress, misery, anger, discontentment, and even revenge over trivial matters in relationships and turn their lives into hell. On the other contrary, being born as a human being is the greatest blessing in itself, meant to be lived happily after realizing the truth.

The following incident from the Indian epic, the Mahabharata illustrates this point and provides valuable lessons.

### The detrimental effect of ego in relationships

This incident relates to Drupad, the king of Panchal, and Dronacharya, the guru of the princes of Hastinapur. In their childhood, they were disciples of the same guru and were very close friends. They learned archery in the guru's hermitage, and their friendship deepened further. Drupad was a prince, while Dronacharya was an ordinary Brahmin. As a child, Drupad had once told Dronacharya, "When I become the king of Panchal, you must stay with me. I will take care of all your comforts. We will always stay together as friends."

To this, Dronacharya replied, "Okay, my dear friend. I also want to always stay with you."

After some years, they completed their education. Drupad grew up to become the king of Panchal. But Dronacharya lived in poverty. Once, his son asked his wife for some milk, but as there was no milk in the house, his wife cried over their plight. Dronacharya was deeply disturbed and pained by this deplorable state.

Then he remembered what his childhood friend Drupad had told him in the past. He considered that he should seek his help in this difficult time. So, he went to meet King Drupad in Panchal. However, King Drupad failed to recognize Dronacharya and insulted him, saying, "How dare you call yourself a friend of the king of Panchal? Look at your status. If you want alms, you will get it. But don't try to fool me in the name of friendship. Otherwise, I will have you put in prison."

With this insult, Dronacharya felt deeply hurt and left quietly. However, this meeting planted the seeds of hatred in his heart for his dearest friend. He resolved that he would surely get his revenge one day.

Time passed and fate favored Dronacharya. He was appointed as the highly revered royal guru of the Kaurava and Pandava princes of Hastinapur. While training all the princes, he realized that Arjuna was the finest archer and most capable among them. Therefore, he specially trained Arjuna in weaponry so that when the time came, Arjuna could help him seek revenge on Drupad.

When the princes completed their education, driven by his desire for revenge, Dronacharya instructed his brave disciple Arjuna to capture Drupad and bring him as his prisoner, as his *Guru-Dakshina*—a homage paid to the guru as a token of respect and gratitude for the guidance received. Accordingly, Arjuna fought a war against King Drupad, defeated him, and presented him as a prisoner before his guru. Having sought his revenge, Dronacharya took away half of Drupad's kingdom, which was the source of his pride, forgave him, and then let him go.

---

**When people realize relationships as a beautiful arrangement made by Nature and learn the art of turning this arrangement into a blessing, their relationships and health will improve.**

---

However, when an insult is retaliated with another insult, it does not end there but intensifies the desire for vengeance. Now, King Drupad couldn't wait to avenge his insult. He performed a great *yajna* (fire sacrifice ritual) and prayed to the gods for an offspring who could take revenge on Dronacharya. Accordingly, two children, Dhrishtadyumna and Draupadi, were born from the flames of the yajna.

This is symbolic of offsprings inheriting the seeds of hatred, borne from the flames of vengeance. History bears witness to how Draupadi played a major role in initiating the battle of Kurukshetra, where King Drupad fulfilled his revenge by having his son, Dhrishtdyumna, kill Dronacharya, thereby getting his revenge.

**The dirt within the layers**

This story depicts how both Dronacharya and Drupad were poisoned by insults and harbored these hurtful scars throughout their lives until they had their revenge against each other. These scars are injured memories. If such injured memories exist within us, they can never let us live a contented life. They keep us sunk in the negative feelings of resentment, anger, and sorrow.

Imagine how King Drupad's life would have been. How happy could he have been as the king of a large empire? Yet, what was his foremost goal? To kill that one person to have his revenge! His life would have been so different had he just agreed to help his friend a little. It would have been such a trivial matter for him, but his pride prevented him from doing so.

Out of sheer arrogance, many of us often choose not to do the good that we can easily do in relationships. For example, if someone does not connect with us, we, too, choose not to connect and care for them. As a result, the gap widens in relationships due to arrogance.

We all have come to this world, and one day, we have to depart. Similarly, Dronacharya also had to leave the world, but King Drupad turned his life into hell due to arrogance. Over the period of many years, so many scars of insult, anger, and revenge accumulated within him, which he passed on to his children and made them instrumental in exacting his revenge.

If we look at the life of King Drupad's daughter Draupadi, she, too, was unhappy. Her entire life was full of struggle, insult, and agony. This is because the primary emotion behind her birth was her father's desire for retaliating revenge, which badly affected his children.

On the other hand, Dronacharya, too, led a life of unhappiness and discontentment. Until he sought revenge on King Drupad, he continued to burn in the fire of insult and vengeance.

Dronacharya was a Brahmin. Just imagine how much knowledge he would have had. What would have happened if he chose to forgive his friend and prayed to God, "O God, my friend is presently unable to see the truth as he is blinded by arrogance. Please grant him wisdom, humility, and love." He could have returned home in peace. With this, there was a possibility that King Drupad would have realized his mistake in the future and corrected himself. Even if King Drupad had not realized his mistake, at least Dronacharya could have led a life of peace and contentment.

Lord Rama and Jesus exemplify sacrifice and forgiveness. In the Indian epic, the Ramayana, Lord Rama peacefully accepted the fourteen-year exile imposed by his stepmother, Queen Kaikeyi. He saw it as divine grace and continued to regard her with love and affection. Even when he had to slay demons, he sought their forgiveness. Similarly, Jesus, while being crucified, asked for forgiveness for those who were crucifying him.

Very often, we tend to blame others for our discontentment in relationships. Whereas, in reality, we are at fault. We must realize that we alone are the root cause of our discontentment, no one else. Therefore, only we can bring ourselves out of disharmony by removing our layers of discontentment.

It is entirely our responsibility to maintain peace, happiness, and contentment in our lives, not someone else's. We must take it up. Let us understand how we can fulfill this responsibility in the next chapter.

**Points for contemplation**

1. Having read about Dronacharya and King Drupad, do you remember any incident from your life where such relationships that were once very dear to you, deteriorated?

2. Reflect on that incident neutrally and examine whether the root cause behind the deterioration of the relationship had been arrogance. What could have been done then to prevent the relationship from being soured?

3. What kind of discontentment do you experience in various relationships? Are there unfulfilled expectations behind them? Can you let go of these expectations?

---

**Case study**

In this chapter, we have read about the scenario between Shivram and his son. What would you advise them so that they can adopt a middle path and lead a life of harmony and contentment?

# 9
# Auspicious Discontentment

The title of this chapter might sound puzzling. How can discontentment be auspicious?! Let us understand this.

When we feel discontented, we often experience negative emotions like anger, sorrow, and stress. To mitigate or escape these uncomfortable emotions, we might seek temporary relief by eating something we like, chatting with friends, browsing social media reels, or shopping. However, these measures only offer short-term respite from our negative emotions.

Is there a better way? There is, but it is seldom chosen. We can allow ourselves to fully experience our negative emotions with awareness and deeply introspect to uncover their root cause. Once identified, we can work on addressing and eradicating these causes to regain our sense of contentment.

During his journeys through the streets of his capital city, Prince Siddhartha experienced deep discontentment after witnessing the four signs of suffering—illness, old age, death, and renunciation. However, he did not try to escape this discontentment by drowning himself in entertainment. Instead, he meditated on the root cause of human suffering and discovered the ultimate way to eradicate it. He became Buddha—the enlightened one. His discontentment was thus auspicious not only for him but also for mankind, as it led him on the path of ultimate liberation.

Like Siddhartha, Vardhamana was also a prince who was raised in royal opulence. Despite having all material wealth at his disposal, he felt deeply discontented. His inner calling led him to undertake severe austerities on the path to ultimate liberation, transforming him into Lord Mahavira.

Chaitanya Mahaprabhu longed for a glimpse of Lord Krishna. This longing led him to experience and revel in the divine presence of the Lord within himself. Similarly, despite acquiring extensive knowledge, Narendra Dutt felt discontented in his early years. This discontentment propelled him toward transcendental wisdom, transforming him into Swami Vivekananda.

> **Discontentment is not always bad. Experiencing discontentment that ultimately drives you toward true contentment is auspicious and far better than settling for mere relief or temporary satisfaction.**

Two friends were traveling by car and met with an accident, where both tragically passed away. Their fathers were deeply shocked and saddened by the incident, wondering why this had happened to them.

One father turned to alcoholism to drown the grief of losing his child. Sadly, he reached a point where he couldn't care for his family anymore. Alcohol only briefly numbed his pain but became a vicious habit, inviting more difficulties in his life.

In contrast, the other father, after grieving for a while, began pondering life's profound questions: What is death? What happens after we die? How does this world function? Why do we get so attached to relationships? These inquiries guided him on the spiritual path. Along this path, he attained wisdom and found answers to his questions. By channeling his sorrow positively, he not only helped himself but also assisted other grieving parents facing similar challenges by establishing a helpline to support them.

Contentment is the essence of our true nature, but the path to its seeking begins with discontentment. The discontentment that drives us on the path of contentment is indeed auspicious!

**How can discontentment be made auspicious?**

Step 1: To give discontentment a positive twist, avoid escaping it through temporary distractions. Instead, identify the root cause of discontentment and write it down. What you can identify, you can resolve more easily.

Step 2: Accept and acknowledge your discontentment and remind yourself, "This feeling is here to teach me something new. I must learn this lesson and continue on my journey of self-development." This will eliminate your inner resistance and make you receptive to the solution for your discontentment.

Step 3: Question and contemplate your discontentment. Asking yourself the right questions leads to the right answers, guiding you onto the right path and freeing you from the cycle of negative emotions like anger, sorrow, and discontentment.

---

**Hidden within any negative incident is a lesson for growth. Once we uncover and learn this lesson through contemplation, we naturally experience true contentment.**

---

Let us understand these three steps from Shivani's story. Shivani was a brilliant student who completed her MBA from a top institute and started working with a Fortune 100 company. Due to her outstanding performance, she rapidly ascended the corporate ladder in five years.

She got married and became pregnant, but complications arose in her pregnancy. Her doctor advised her to either abort the child or leave her job and remain on complete bed rest to continue the pregnancy.

The emerging mother within Shivani chose the second option. She left her job and took complete bed rest during her pregnancy. Due to complications, she delivered her child prematurely at seven months. The baby was very weak. Shivani could not consider re-joining her job after the delivery as her child's health and well-being became her top priority.

Shivani took on the full responsibility of caring for her child, but as months rolled by, she grew restless and discontented. Seeing her friends, colleagues, and batchmates progress on social media—earning higher salaries, advancing in their careers, and traveling the world—left her feeling frustrated and trapped within the four walls of her house.

She often wondered why she had taken on the responsibility of marriage and if it was worth it. While she was happy that her child was well cared for and healthy, the way her career had taken a backseat made her extremely discontented. Her mood frequently soured, leading to arguments with Vijay, her husband. She often told him, "We are both responsible for our child. Then, why do I have to sacrifice my career while yours continues to progress as before?"

She often spoke to her parents and old friends and ordered food she enjoyed, all to lift her mood. Yet, these activities brought only temporary relief, and her feeling of discontentment persisted as a constant undercurrent. Over time, this ongoing discontentment turned into depression.

Then Shivani came across the three-step method we discussed earlier.

The first step was for her to write down why she was repeatedly feeling restless and discontented. She needed to uncover her true feelings behind these emotions.

Shivani wrote down the following answer: "When I see my friends and colleagues progressing in their professional lives, I feel left behind. I deeply regret sacrificing my career. I believe it is now nearly impossible to catch up and achieve the heights I could have attained if I hadn't left my job. I also feel frustrated because I had to make this sacrifice alone while Vijay continues to grow in his career."

Then, she took the second step. With a calm mind, she told herself, "I fully accept my feeling of discontentment. This feeling has come to show me a new path and teach me something. I must learn this lesson and move toward growth."

In the third step, Shivani began to inquire within herself, "Why am I so frustrated?" The answer emerged, "Because I had to stop doing the work I loved. As a result, I lost my passion and sense of self-identity."

She asked herself a second question: "Whose decision was it to leave the job? Was anyone forcing me to make this decision? What did I gain from leaving my job?"

On deep reflection, she received the following answers: "It was my decision to leave my job. No one forced me to make that choice. After leaving my job, I gained the life of my child, whom I love so dearly."

Then she asked herself: "Why do I feel that the life I am leading is meaningless?"

She had to meditate deeply on this question, and the answer she eventually uncovered surprised her. The root cause was a belief she had borrowed during her childhood: "Being a housewife and caring for the family is less meaningful than being a working woman. A working woman always has value and identity, whereas simply being a housewife is considered to have no value." This belief was at the heart of her frustration. She found her current role as a homemaker worthless.

She also discovered another reason for her frustration. She had genuinely loved the work she had done and wanted to continue doing it. Then she asked herself, "Is there any way I can both care for my child and continue doing the work I love?"

She researched the subject and found a solution. Leveraging her expertise, she began teaching online as a guest lecturer at various national and international management institutes. This move revitalized her connection to her field of work, dispelling her depression. It also provided her with income while ensuring her child received proper care.

Shivani loved teaching so much that after four years, she started her own coaching firm, which quickly gained popularity. Over time, she established a significant reputation in academics. She earned more than she would have in a traditional job, and her flexible working hours allowed her to balance work and family responsibilities effectively. In this way, the three correct steps taken by Shivani gave a positive twist to her discontentment, leading her to a path of great success.

Asking ourselves simple yet insightful questions can often guide us on the right path in life. Therefore, when we face sorrow, frustration, or discontentment, it is important to acknowledge and accept these feelings and then pose the right questions to ourselves for self-introspection.

**Points for contemplation**

1. If you are feeling frustrated or discontented in any present situation, take the first step by writing down the root cause and the underlying emotions on paper. Next, accept your frustration and discontentment as the second step.

2. Then, ask yourself the right questions and engage in self-introspection. Write down the answers and aim to steer yourself toward a new pathway.

3. Finally, assess your feelings. Have you successfully redirected your discontentment? If not, continue questioning yourself and practicing deeper self-introspection until you find clarity and a new direction.

> **Case study**
>
> You have learned about Shivani's situation in this chapter. If you were to advise Shivani again, which new dimensions and possibilities would you explore for her circumstances?

# 10
# Feel Contented by Making Others Contented

Once there was a king whose subjects were very happy with his governance. He maintained good relations with neighboring kingdoms, and his kingdom was continuously flourishing. Everyone in that kingdom was proud of their king.

However, the king was not content. He felt that something was missing but couldn't figure out what it was.

One day, the king went to his guru with this question. His guru said, "The best way to attain something that we don't have is to help others attain it. Then that thing will naturally come to us. For example, if you want happiness, strive to make others happy. This will augment happiness in your own life as well. Similarly, if you seek contentment, do something for others that will make them feel content."

The guru instructed the king to remove the lack from the life of the first person he would meet the next day morning and make him feel contented. By doing this, the king would also feel contented.

The king followed the guru's instructions. The next morning, when he was riding on his chariot, he saw a beggar standing beside a drain. He thought, "How pitiable the beggar's condition is! If I give him a silver coin early in the morning, he will surely be happy." He took out a silver coin from his purse and tossed it in the direction of the beggar, saying, "Hey, take this coin, go home and relax."

The beggar was very happy to see the silver coin. He tried to catch it, but unfortunately, it fell into the drain.

The king realized his mistake. He took another coin from his purse, and this time, he got down from his chariot and started walking toward the beggar to place the coin directly in his hand. By then, the beggar had started trying to retrieve the coin from the drain.

The king stopped the beggar and said, "Hey, why are you getting into the drain? I will give you two coins instead. Take them and go home."

The beggar happily accepted the two coins and kept them in his pocket. The king was about to leave. However, when he turned back, he was in for a surprise. He saw that the beggar was once again trying to retrieve the coin from the drain.

He thought, "My guru had instructed me to make someone contented but here, the beggar is not content with even two coins."

He walked up to the beggar again, gave him four more silver coins, and said, "Look, I have given you four times more than the value of the fallen coin. So, forget about the fallen coin. Don't go back to the drain."

The beggar folded his hands and replied to the king, "Your Majesty, you are very kind. I do agree that you have given me four times more than the value of the fallen coin, but my mind is still stuck on the same coin. I will not be content until I retrieve it from the drain. After all, you gave me that coin. Now, it belongs to me, and I cannot leave behind anything that is rightfully mine."

The king was startled upon hearing this and thought, "Why not give the beggar so much wealth that he won't think about that coin anymore? Perhaps, then he will feel content."

The king told the beggar, "I will give you this bag full of coins. Now, forget about that coin and go home." The beggar replied, "Your Majesty, even then, after going back home, my mind would still be stuck on that one coin lying in the drain."

The king asked the beggar, "Is that the case? If I give you half my kingdom, will you return home contented?"

The beggar replied, "Sure, I will go away from here, provided you give me that half part of your kingdom which contains this drain!"

On hearing this reply, the king got frustrated. He bowed to the beggar, placed the bag of coins in his hands, left him to his situation, and departed.

So, what do we learn from this story?

We cannot make someone contented until they feel content in their perspectives and thoughts. As long as they remain attached to the coin lying in the drain, they will continue to feel discontented. Even if they have everything, they will find something missing that will make them discontented. Hence, never feel sad or discontented because you cannot make someone else contented.

Though the king could help others, it was not in his power to make them contented. On the other hand, he alone could make himself contented provided he worked on his own beliefs and perspectives. If he focussed on the abundance that he was blessed with instead of the fallen coin in his life, he would feel grateful and contented.

People in offices and at home often feel troubled and sad because no matter how hard they work for others, others are never satisfied with them. They make every possible effort to make others happy, yet others find some fault or another. Hence, we must restrain ourselves from attempting to satisfy everyone in our lives.

We must perform the deeds that ought to be done. Fulfill our responsibilities without imposing the condition or harboring the desire that others should be content. Otherwise, this very thought will become the cause of our discontentment.

We must always continue to extend love, happiness, and service to others, whether our actions make them feel contented or not. We should do such things for others that will enable them to choose light, wisdom, and the right path in their life.

For example, you see some acquaintances struggling due to lack of money. One way is to help them by giving money. Another way is to help them become self-sufficient or do something that can increase their income. You work toward creating a new opportunity for them. You gift them a book that could help them learn money management.

Suppose you give them money. When they run out of money, they will be stranded in the same situation as before, and you will not feel content seeing them. However, if you teach them to earn money and watch them progress in life, you will feel more contented and happier. In other words, you don't need to feed fish to the needy every day; instead, you need to teach them how to fish.

Those who seize the initiative to help others and work for their welfare, always remain very happy and contented.

**Points for contemplation**

1. Have you ever experienced contentment by helping a stranger by giving them something or empowering them?
2. Contemplate whether your mind is stuck into something trivial as the beggar did. Is that the cause of your discontentment? Can you let go of that desire?
3. Try at least once a day or once a week to make someone feel content.

### Case study

Divya's friends commute to college on motor-scooters, so she asks her father to buy her a motor-scooter. She insists on this demand to such an extent that she becomes despondent. On the other hand, her father cannot afford to buy her a scooter due to his financial condition. On one hand, there is an insistence, and on the other hand, there is a situation in which both Divya and her father are discontented. What would you advise them so that they can feel content?

# PART II

# UNDERSTANDING TRUE CONTENMENT

# 11
## The Magical Feeling of Havingness

There is a popular hymn in Hindi that translates as –

*The poor find the rich happy, the rich find the King;*
*The King finds the Emperor happy, the Emperor finds Gods;*
*Gods find Lord Rama happy, Lord Rama finds saints;*
*Saints find bliss in contentment, free from suffering due to discontent.*

Everyone defines happiness differently. We often feel we lack something others have, believing it makes them happy. True happiness lies in contentment, which surpasses all other forms of happiness.

Now, we need to work on this feeling that prevents us from experiencing contentment and gives us a sense of lack. The sense of "something is missing" underlies all forms of discontentment. We need to find ways to overcome this sense of lack.

When someone sees a half-filled glass, they might say, "The glass is half empty." Although what they are saying is true, there is also the possibility of filling up the remaining half. Those who do not see the empty half but focus on the possibility of filling it indicate to nature that they are open to receiving blessings. This attitude helps them move toward contentment.

We also need to see this possibility. To do so, we must first learn not to place an order of "lack" to nature, even by mistake.

**What is the order of "lack"?**

If someone were asked to list all the things for which they are grateful to God, they might mention a few things. However, if asked about what they haven't received, they could come up with a long list or even write an essay about what they lack in life.

People often call each other to complain about what they have not received or what they lack. For instance, they might talk about not getting enough time to finish work, not getting enough rest, not having a maid for household chores, not getting a promotion, not enjoying a movie they watched, not finding a seat at a restaurant, not finding peace at a crowded hill-station, or not getting enough likes and comments on their social media posts.

Thus, the entire conversation is focused on what they lack. It is nature's law that what we focus on gets attracted into our life. So, when we focus on what we lack, we attract even more lack into our lives.

Two friends were eating gol-gappas, a tangy Indian snack. While one relished it, the other hesitated, "It's a rainy day. I am not sure whether I should eat gol-gappas. I hope it doesn't affect my throat like last time." Two days later, her throat did become sore, while the other friend was fine. She remarked, "See, I knew my throat would get irritated after eating gol-gappas!"

How did she know it beforehand? This is because she invited the illness with her powerful thoughts and focus. While eating gol-gappas, her mind was fixated on one thought, "My throat should not become sore." Her intense focus attracted what she was thinking into her life.

Knowingly or unknowingly, we attract good and bad things into our lives through our attention and thoughts. When we focus on what we lack, we unknowingly block things that were meant to come into our lives according to our divine plan.

Someone who says, "No matter how much I try to take care, I always fall sick," can never be healthy. Those who continuously lament the lack of money can never prosper. Those who say, "I always succeed only after a great struggle. I never succeed easily like others," invite more struggle into their lives.

Nature is always quietly blessing us, "So be it!" Whatever we feel deep within, manifests in our lives.

Therefore, instead of searching for the cause of our discontentment outside, and blaming others or our fate, we must resolve to shift our focus from the feeling of lack to a feeling of "havingness."

Let us understand the feeling of havingness and how we can experience it.

**The feeling of havingness**

The feeling of havingness is the feeling of abundance. It implies having conviction in the truth that everything is available in abundance for everyone. Nature has everything in abundance for everyone; there is no lack anywhere. This is the truth, but people find it difficult to believe. They focus more on what is lacking in their lives or the lives of others around them. They think, "If so many people in the world are suffering from scarcity and poverty, how can we experience the feeling of abundance?"

When rain pours over the entire city, does everyone get drenched? Does everyone receive rainwater? Although the clouds shower abundant water on everyone without bias, only those who have not confined themselves within the four walls or have not shielded themselves under their umbrellas receive the rainwater. The feeling of lack is symbolized by the umbrella or house, which prevents them from getting drenched in the rain of Nature's abundance.

Some people keep saying, "It's hard to find good people these days. There is a dearth of good, noble people in this world." This belief hinders them, preventing good, noble people from appearing in their lives.

A person had a strong belief since childhood that "I always get very good, honest friends in my life." His belief truly attracted good, honest friends throughout his life. With their help, he could easily overcome the toughest of circumstances in his life. On the other hand, his brother always thought, "My brother has such good friends, but I don't have any." Unknowingly, he developed that belief and prevented good friends from entering his life.

In this way, many people have held their umbrellas of negative beliefs open, which prevents them from enjoying Nature's bountiful showers. Some examples are, "Money does not stay with me," "If I feel well for two days, I fall sick on the third day," "I always get betrayed in friendships and relationships," and so on.

In this case, first and foremost, remove the feeling of lack and replace it with the feeling of havingness. This can happen with firm belief. Nature says, "Have faith, dwell in the feeling of abundance, bring about inner change, and then the outside scene will automatically change for the better." Thus, the person says, "First, show me the proof, then I will believe," and Nature says, "Start believing, and you will get the proof."

Let us understand it this way. The human brain is divided into two parts: the left brain and the right brain. The left brain thinks analytically and has the habit of reasoning out everything based on its logic. It prefers to see everything logically. Therefore, it first asks for evidence before choosing to believe in anything. On the other hand, the right brain is creative, intuitive, and illogical. It can believe in things seemingly illogical. For example, a two-year-old child acts solely based on faith without any logic.

Similarly, Nature also operates in an illogical manner. It tells us, "First believe, then you will receive evidence." Hence, first, raise your faith using your right brain. Develop a strong faith that there is abundant love in relationships, good health, peace, prosperity, success, and creativity. If you cultivate these feelings first, everything else is bound to come.

As you change your feelings, Nature will reciprocate. You will start seeing the evidence in due course. But until then, patiently hold on to your feeling of havingness.

---

> Happiness and contentment are not worldly things to be acquired. They are the qualities of our divine essence to be realized as the supreme goal of life.

---

### Affirm to yourself with full faith

- I have abundant time for good things, for doing good work, for my family, and for fulfilling my dreams.
- I am always in perfect health. I am filled with positive, divine energy.
- Success, prosperity, and abundance are easily flowing in my life according to my divine plan.
- All my relationships are filled with harmony, love, respect, and trust.
- I am filled with divine virtues like love, bliss, peace, and compassion.
- I am able to fully receive the divine grace abundantly showered on me.

In this manner, sow the seeds of abundance within and witness miracles unfolding in your life.

### Points for contemplation

1. In which areas of your life do you feel a lack, or abundance? For example, health, wealth, relationships, talent, skills, success at work, physical beauty, intelligence, respect, etc.

2. In the areas where you feel a lack, when did you start experiencing those feelings? Were they sensed right from the beginning, or did they arise after specific circumstances? Get rid of the feeling and memory of such incidents with the "Let go" mantra.

3. In the areas where you feel a lack, keep yourself in the feeling of havingness with full faith. Affirm to yourself with full faith, "Everything is in abundance." Thank God for the areas where you feel abundance. By expressing gratitude, it multiplies further.

4. Write down the affirmations that are relevant to you and repeat them regularly.

### Case study

A youth named Satish comes to you and says, "I am hardly able to save money. Just when I get my salary on payday every month, I get a call from home stating, "We need this," "We need that," or "Someone is sick," and I spend all my money on them. I work so hard that I toil even during holidays. I am hardly ever happy. I do so much for everyone, but no one does anything for me. What can I do?"

What would you advise Satish in this situation? What magical feeling would you pass on to him?

# 12
# All Our Needs Are Being Fulfilled

True contentment is experienced by those who believe their present needs are being fulfilled and trust that their future needs will also be met. Nature takes care of them now and will continue to do so. If a specific need is not met right now, it means it is not necessary at the moment. The non-fulfillment of this need is exactly what is required at present. If it is meant to be a need in the future, it will indeed be fulfilled at the right time, and that future can come at any time.

Let us understand this with an example. Ravi worked in a factory that manufactured electric bulbs. He was skilled and honest, and the owner was very pleased with him. Ravi never took leaves and worked diligently, leading the owner to increase his salary significantly. However, Ravi was forced to take leave right after his salary hike. As he managed much of the company's work alone, his absence left many tasks pending, resulting in huge losses.

Seeing this, the company owner was annoyed. He thought, "I praised him and increased his salary, and it has gone to his head. When he returns, I will lower his salary so he will never repeat this mistake."

After returning from leave, Ravi continued to work diligently as before. When he received a lesser salary on payday, he did not say anything to anyone and continued to work with the same diligence.

After two months, Ravi again took leave. The company owner thought, "Now Ravi is deliberately trying to create problems because I reduced his salary. He wants me to suffer losses." So, he further reduced Ravi's salary, but this did not affect Ravi. He continued to work with the same diligence as before.

The owner wondered, "Whether I increased or decreased Ravi's salary, he quietly worked with the same focus and diligence. Most people's behavior would have changed completely if I had done this to them."

One day, the owner could no longer contain his curiosity and asked Ravi, "When I raised your salary, you didn't show any joy. When I reduced it, you didn't show any sorrow or anger. Your behavior remained the same in both situations. How is this possible?"

Ravi responded, "Immediately after you raised my salary, my son was born. It made me feel like God was taking care of me. My family grew, and my salary increased. The second time I took leave was when my mother passed away. She had been ill for a while, and we had spent a lot on her treatment. When she passed away, the medical expenses were reduced, and so was my salary. I realized that if God is managing my affairs, why should I worry? He adjusts my salary based on my needs. What greater contentment could there be than this?"

The owner was amazed by Ravi's response. He had always celebrated small profits and deeply mourned losses, unaware that life could be approached as Ravi did. Despite his wealth and possessions, he had never known true contentment. Inspired by Ravi, the owner prayed, "O God, please manage my affairs as you do for Ravi. I surrender my worries and needs to you. From now on, please provide what I truly need." After this, the owner, too, began to experience genuine contentment in his life.

**There is no other, and nothing is ever missing.**

The above line is the mantra that embodies true contentment. "There is no other" implies that we must see everyone as a part of ourselves without seeing anyone as separate. Let us always celebrate the successes and joys of others as if they were our own. By doing so, we can avoid envy and comparison, and invite more success, happiness, and contentment into our lives.

"Nothing is ever missing" signifies that whatever we truly need in our lives right now is already here. If something seems absent, its absence itself is what we need at this moment.

People often view life from a limited and shortsighted perspective. They focus on what they perceive as missing or lacking and keep thinking, "This is missing… That's not available…" Yet, when viewed from a higher birds-eye view, we realize that if anything is absent in our lives right now, its absence is precisely what we need at this moment.

We often hear rags-to-riches stories, but there are also riches-to-rags stories of wealthy families who fall into poverty due to accidents or business losses. Their next generation, accustomed to luxury, have to suddenly adapt to a humbled, deprived lifestyle. These experiences offer them invaluable lessons that serve them well, which their previous wealth could never have taught them.

We benefit from the presence of some things, while certain things benefit us through their absence in our lives, though we may not see it right away. It is only in hindsight, through reflection and introspection, that we realize how whatever was missing or the challenges we faced have helped shape where we are today.

---

**Incidents will occur in our lives as they are meant to be, but we should continue to pray for the kind of future we wish for—a life filled with love, happiness, peace, wonder, and contentment.**

---

Rajiv wanted to pursue post-graduation after completing his degree, but his father's demise forced him to work as a salesman to support his family. Saddened by the need to discontinue his studies, he struggled to focus on his work. Stress and discontentment plagued him, often leading to sleepless nights that he spent scrolling aimlessly on his phone.

One day, his mother scolded him, saying, "You waste so much time on your phone; you might as well read a good book and increase your knowledge." This sparked an idea in Rajiv. He enrolled for his post-graduation through private study and began studying at night.

He now dedicated the time he once spent surfing the internet and watching reels on social media to studying and completing his post-graduation. After finishing his studies, he was promoted in his job and felt contented. With this accomplishment, he was finally able to sleep well at night.

One day, he thanked God and said, "Thank God I lost sleep back then; otherwise, I wouldn't have completed my post-graduation!"

This is how the Divine plan works for us. If we feel something is missing in our lives, let us reflect on the lesson God might be teaching us through this absence. What new opportunities are emerging because of it? Once we grasp this, we will understand why it was necessary for that thing to remain absent.

Some things we may understand, and some we may not—but God knows everything. This is why we should always trust the divine orchestra of our lives, believing that God is meeting every necessary need. With this faith, discontentment will have no place within us.

**Points for contemplation**

1. Do you feel that all your present needs are being fulfilled? If not, which needs do you think are still unfulfilled?
2. For those needs you feel are unfulfilled, consider whether they truly need to be fulfilled right now. Could their absence be necessary for this moment in your life?

3. Reflect on your past to see if there were unfulfilled needs that rendered your life meaningless. What lessons did you learn because those needs were not met?
4. How has the fulfillment of past needs impacted your life? Do you feel content now, or have new needs drawn your attention?
5. Have you developed any new strengths or skills due to the non-fulfillment of your past needs?
6. Reflect deeply on the mantra: "There is no other, and nothing is ever missing."

---

**Case study**

Rohan has been working with a software company for seven years. Today, he expected to receive his annual salary increment, but he didn't get the raise for some reason. He felt deeply hurt and spent the day cursing his boss. He believed his hard work over the last year was in vain, and his life is meaningless. He even considered resigning immediately.

Now, you meet Rohan and invite him over to guide him toward clarity and contentment. What questions would you ask Rohan to help him gain a better perspective?

# 13
# Finding Contentment Through Forgiveness

We are intricately linked to several relationships and engage in karmic transactions with many people. As a result, disagreements inevitably arise; either they hurt us, or we hurt them, knowingly or unknowingly.

These karmic transactions accumulate within us in the form of scars, which get triggered from time to time, making us feel sad and perturbed. If we make decisions under their influence, we will suffer similar consequences as King Drupad and Guru Dronacharya did.

Forgiveness is like cool water that can extinguish the fire of all kinds of vices and karmic scars, bringing happiness and contentment in every relationship.

Those who think that forgiving others is not always easy must read the story below.

### Calmness through forgiveness

While preaching on the importance of contentment and forgiveness in life, a saint said, "There is one path to success and happiness in life – forgiveness and contentment."

A disciple asked him, "Gurudev, if someone insults another, then how can one forgive them?"

The saint smiled and said, "When someone hurts another, a negative feeling arises within them. This disrupts their inner peace and leaves them with a feeling of missing or lack, which keeps them away from contentment. The only way to dispel this feeling of missing is to practice forgiveness which brings contentment. In short, when we forgive someone or ask someone for forgiveness, we are not doing a favor on them. Rather, we are healing our karmic scars that relieve our own burden. We start feeling contented from within.

"Therefore, forgiving or seeking forgiveness are considered great virtues in life. When we forgive someone, we touch the pinnacle of contentment. The path of forgiveness and contentment helps us progress toward peace and happiness, which is the true wealth of life."

**Forgiveness is a double-edged sword**

Forgiveness works both ways. The one who seeks forgiveness becomes free from sorrow and discontentment. Similarly, the one who forgives also remains free.

Besides forgiving others, we can also forgive ourselves. Many times, we harbor guilt for ourselves. Possibly, we inadvertently committed a mistake in an emotional state, which caused us to feel guilty. We repeatedly think about it, feel sad, and rebuke ourselves for this. We should stop doing this. After realizing our mistakes, we should forgive ourselves and resolve not to repeat them.

For example, a man spoke very rudely to his mother in anger. On realizing his mistake, he asked for forgiveness from his mother but could not forgive himself. He kept thinking, "How could I speak to my mother like that?" This thought became the cause of sorrow and stress within him.

---

**It takes courage to seek forgiveness and a big heart to forgive.**

---

We are all humans, not robots. Often, we become overwhelmed by our emotions. We may be annoyed by something but vent this anger on someone else, especially those close to us. Sometimes, we lose control over our responses. In such instances, we must be alert and aware, and seek forgiveness without being rude on ourselves.

Earth is like a school where we have come to learn our lessons. While learning these lessons, we may commit some mistakes. Everyone is on their journey of training. It is not wrong to make mistakes. Everyone learns their lessons over time. Therefore, do not hold onto others' hurtful words as well as yours. Use the duster of forgiveness as soon as possible to erase the mental dirt that is causing you sorrow and discontentment.

**How to practice forgiveness**

Once you realize your mistake while dealing with someone, first accept your mistake. If you are comfortable with directly seeking forgiveness from someone, then seek forgiveness in person, saying, "Please forgive me for the sorrow I caused you through my feelings, thoughts, words, or actions. I will ensure that I will not repeat this mistake again." At least in close relationships, directly seek forgiveness.

There may be instances where you may not be comfortable seeking forgiveness directly, or you may realize your mistakes much later. In such cases, mentally seek forgiveness from that person and forgive them by inviting them into your field of awareness. Similarly, invite yourself into your field of awareness and forgive yourself. When you learn to forgive yourself, you will be able to forgive others easily.

After consistently practicing forgiveness, you will see miraculous results in your life. You will wonder, "Those who weren't speaking to me directly have started changing their behavior toward me. Relationships are becoming harmonious. Problems are getting resolved. Everything is beginning to flow spontaneously in life. Inner peace and contentment are rising."

In this way, remove the accumulated scars within with the practice of forgiveness and bring contentment in relationships.

**Points for contemplation**

1. Remember someone who makes you feel angry. Accept your feelings toward them.
2. Tell yourself, "They are right in their place, and I am right in mine." With this feeling, invite them into your field of awareness. Forgive them from the bottom of your heart and welcome contentment.
3. Invite yourself into your field of awareness and forgive yourself for all those things you have harbored within, like guilt or resentment. Tell yourself, "I have learned my lesson from this mistake. I will not repeat it. I forgive myself and release all thoughts related to this mistake."
4. Develop a firm belief that mindfully choosing your responses in small incidents fosters your inner strength, which is a significant step toward contentment.

---

**Case study**

In the example in Chapter 8, Shivram spoke harshly to his newlywed son and daughter-in-law and asked them to leave the house. He also removed them from his will, creating deep karmic scars in the process. Many relatives tried to counsel them but ended up feeling hurt themselves. Knowing this background, how would you guide them?

## 14

## Choosing Contentment in Adversity

Once, there were massive riots in a city. Hearing this, a grocer locked up his store and headed home. On his way, he heard that the rioters had set fire to his house. Upon hearing this, he laughed and thanked God.

People thought he couldn't handle the bad news and had gone mad. They tried to console him, but he replied, "I am truly happy, which is why I am laughing. Just yesterday, my wife and children travelled to her parent's town, and there were no servants at home when this happened. I am grateful to God for protecting us from this incident. I am so happy."

The grocer returned home and managed to put out the fire. Then he received news that the rioters had looted his shop. Once again, he laughed and thanked God. When asked why, he replied, "I had already delivered more than half of my stock to customers yesterday, and the remaining half hasn't arrived at my store yet due to the riots. The little stock left in the store was just basic groceries. Even if someone took them away, it's okay."

The next day, the riots had stopped, and the grocer went to his store. He noticed there was still some ration left in a corner. Once again, he laughed and thanked God, saying, "O God, your grace is infinite! Even in these tough circumstances, you have set aside some ration for me for the next few days. You care so much for me!" Then he happily collected the remaining ration and returned home.

**Let happiness and contentment be our choice**

If one decides to remain happy and content under any circumstance, no one can take their happiness and contentment away.

From the above story, one might think, "This is insanity! Who can remain happy and peaceful after facing such adverse circumstances?" They may be right because, in today's world, people often brood over the most trivial things and complain even when they have everything they need in life. In such a context, if someone chooses to laugh in the face of adversity, their behavior seems very odd to others.

This is why people regard contentment, peace, and joy as a rarity in present times. Instead, stress and anger are more readily accepted as normal. When we see someone genuinely content and happy, we often think they are insane, impractical, or faking it. Unable to accept that one can be genuinely happy and content, people justify their incorrect beliefs by coining proverbs like: "A person who laughs excessively hides some deep sorrow within."

However, there are still some rare people like the grocer who can laugh under adverse circumstances. Such people are not swayed by adversity. They have trained themselves to remain happy in every situation by making a clear choice and consistently practicing this attitude in their lives.

If we also make a clear choice that **"No matter what happens, I will never compromise on my happiness,"** then this is indeed possible. In adverse circumstances, we have two choices: We can either focus on what we lack or take an overall view of our situation and feel grateful for what we have, as the grocer did. By choosing gratitude, even in tough times, we can eliminate the feeling of lack and experience contentment.

Initially, it may be challenging to practice gratitude immediately, especially in adverse circumstances. However, if we train ourselves to cultivate daily gratitude for everything we have in our lives, it becomes easier to maintain this practice during tough times and overcome the feeling of lack more effectively.

A scientist was conducting an experiment that seemed unsolvable. While he was working, his dog barged into the laboratory and destroyed the entire setup. The scientist's helper feared his anger for allowing the dog in. Surprisingly, the scientist gently patted the dog and said, "Thank you, my friend, you've saved me! I was struggling to figure out the next step in the experiment. Now, I can start anew and try a completely different approach. Perhaps I'll succeed this time."

Two people may face the same adverse circumstance, yet their responses can differ significantly. How someone responds in difficult times depends on their preparedness, perspective on life, and their choices. Those who habitually choose happiness, peace, and contentment will likely make decisions aligned with these values even in adversity.

---

**Deeds performed without selfish interest eventually yield the ultimate fruit of supreme contentment.**

---

## The harmful effect of incorrect choices

Although circumstances may be beyond our control, how we respond to them is within our power. It is essential always to choose responses that benefit us in every situation. Getting angry, becoming sad or depressed, and feeling discontented are inferior choices that lead to adverse outcomes. Sometimes, the adversity we face may not be as harmful as the negative consequences we bring upon ourselves by making incorrect choices.

Two friends took a competitive exam, but both failed. One chose to stay positive, study harder, and attempt the exam again. The other turned to drugs to cope with his sorrow. The first friend eventually passed the exam after two years and succeeded. Meanwhile, the second friend's life spiraled out of control due to his poor choice of response.

Both friends were equally talented, yet they made different choices when faced with adversity. Failing the exam did not have as severe a consequence as one friend's decision to drown his sorrow in drugs. This underscores the importance of making a clear decision beforehand: Regardless of circumstances, we must never compromise our happiness and contentment.

Someone who is constantly discontented with their ill health often seeks external solutions, asking everyone they meet about treatments or recommendations for a good doctor. If someone were to suggest to them, "The cure you seek is already within you. If you stop worrying and start laughing, good health will naturally be attracted into your life," they would likely not believe it.

But it is indeed true. Medical research has demonstrated the adverse side effects on our bodies when we experience anger or other negative emotions for even a short period like 5 minutes. These emotions can significantly impact our cardiovascular and digestive systems. While a brief period of negativity might not cause severe harm, habitual negativity can attract serious chronic diseases that can profoundly affect our health over time.

After understanding this, we should believe in maintaining happiness and laughter even in adverse circumstances, similar to the grocer who chose to be happy despite his home burning down and store being looted. When our health and mindset are optimistic and resilient, we can easily confront even the most challenging situations. Therefore, when faced with adversity, let us take our first step toward overcoming it with laughter.

**Points for contemplation**

1. Reflect on the impact of negative emotions on your body. Have you experienced side effects like insomnia, indigestion, acidity, or headaches after feeling angry, stressed, or worried?

2. Recall a time when you were unwell but still felt happy. Did your illness affect you adversely? When you were happy despite being unwell, did you feel physically worse or more contented and at ease with your health condition?

3. In the future, if you ever face adversity, first laugh and then tell yourself, "I am always in favor of happiness and contentment. My laughter will always give me the strength to overcome any problem."

---

**Case study**

"No matter what happens, I will never compromise on my happiness." Make your own narrative based on this sentence in the context of any challenge you face. (Narrative therapy helps to distance oneself from one's problems by externalizing them instead of internalizing them.)

# 15
## Finding Contentment Through Patience

Karan was a talented actor. He aspired to move to Mumbai and become a star in the film industry. To achieve this, he made extensive preparations, taking acting courses and improving his personality and skills.

However, he was plagued by negative thoughts. He worried about the struggle in Mumbai, where he would stay, and how soon he would get his big break in the film industry.

Karan took the train to Mumbai and started staying as a paying guest. After a few days, he got a call for an audition scheduled in two weeks. During this period, he was overwhelmed with anxiety and restlessness, constantly assailed by negative thoughts: "Will I be selected at the audition? What should I do next? How should I do it?" Those two weeks felt like an eternity to him.

The day of the audition arrived, and it went well. However, the results would be known only after four weeks. Karan found it very difficult to pass the next month. He was again flooded with negative thoughts: "Will I be selected? What will I do if I'm rejected?" Lost in these thoughts, he remained restless and discontented.

After a long month of anxious wait, Karan's dreams finally came true. He got selected for the role he had auditioned for and finally got his first break in the film industry. While he felt momentarily relieved and satisfied, he also felt the immense pressure of proving himself as a good actor. He knew that if he succeeded in his first movie, more opportunities would follow. However, he also continued to worry about the possibility of failure.

Two years later, his film was released and became a blockbuster. Yet, he remained uneasy, concerned about the next role he would be offered.

Given his disposition, it seems unlikely that Karan's discontentment would ever end. This is because he had not learned to cultivate patience during the time between his work and its results.

Many people believe that only unsuccessful individuals are discontented, while successful ones are contented. But this is not entirely true. Contentment is our inherent virtue. Those who have it remain contented regardless of any circumstances. Otherwise, one can never feel contented, even when everything is fine in life. This discontentment often stems from a sense of missing or lack.

When we have completed our work and await the results, a peculiar sense of "missing" often creeps in, allowing negative thoughts to take hold. These negative thoughts contribute to a heightened sense of lack, making contentment elusive. This is why it is crucial to counter negative thoughts by reminding ourselves, "I've given my absolute best," and embrace this mindset. Doing so helps us break free from feelings of inadequacy and gradually cultivate contentment.

### The key of patience

Successful and hardworking individuals can still experience discontentment when they lack patience. The quality of their lives hinges on how they manage the time between their efforts and the outcomes. Trying to rush through this period or feeling restless prevents true contentment from gracing their lives.

Life should be approached like playing the piano. A pianist creates beautiful music by pressing the right keys at the right time, neither too quickly nor too slowly. In the same way, life unfolds best when we act with poise and balance. Each action requires the right amount of effort, akin to pressing the keys with the correct pressure.

However, people succumb to impatience, striving to rush through tasks. Just as playing the piano in a hurry produces discordant music, hastiness in life leads to disharmony and discontentment. Trying to speed up does not accelerate outcomes. Everything unfolds naturally in its own time. **Embracing patience and balance is vital to fostering positivity and contentment in life.**

Some musicians do not find satisfaction in their own performance, nor do their audiences. They lack harmony and attunement with their art. Some other musicians may please their audiences with their performance but feel dissatisfied themselves, believing they could have done better. This leaves them dissatisfied while stepping off the stage, i.e., they depart the world feeling discontented.

Then, there are musicians whose performances delight both themselves and the audiences. However, they struggle with consistency and spend much of their lives feeling discontented. This inconsistency stems from their inability to exercise patience and contentment with every performance.

To experience true contentment, we must strive to be like the best musicians in every circumstance, mastering the art of being contented regardless of external events. We should train ourselves to maintain our composure and satisfaction, no matter what happens around us.

In the first example of this chapter, if Karan had focused solely on his performance and surrendered the outcome to the divine will, he would have found happiness and contentment in any situation. His joy and satisfaction would come from giving his best performance, not its outcome.

In the Bhagavad Gita, Lord Krishna teaches us that we must continue to play the flute of patience, peace, and contentment in times of adversity. We should train ourselves to live in such a way that we can maintain this inner harmony and a sense of self-assurance even under the most challenging circumstances.

Lord Krishna said, "There is no duty that I am obliged to do, and I am not bound by any deed. Though I perform deeds with enthusiasm, yet I remain detached from them. I am neither attached to the success of any endeavor nor do I suffer from its failure. I remain steadfast, peaceful, and fully contented in doing what is worthy, and yet remain a non-doer."

We should also strive to live like Lord Krishna, playing the sweet music of contentment under any circumstance.

---

**When we become impatient for the result of our actions, we forget our true nature. Therefore, learn to be patient and rise above petty desires, focusing on the ultimate purpose of human life—to be established in our true nature.**

---

### Wait, watch with wonder

A lady's son was returning home by cab from another city, two years after completing his studies. Due to bad weather and a poor network connection, she couldn't reach him by phone. This filled her with negative thoughts: "Why hasn't he reached home yet? I hope nothing has happened to him!" Her worry turned into impatience and restlessness, and she began praying to God for her son's safe arrival.

After some time, her son sent her a message with the live location of his cab. She could now see exactly where the cab was on the map and how long it would take him to reach home. This relieved her greatly. She stopped worrying and instead waited joyfully for his arrival.

The weather remained bad, and her son encountered a traffic jam, prolonging his journey home. Despite this, his mother remained unworried. She kept track of his cab's progress on the map and reassured herself, **"Since he is already on his way, he will surely arrive in due course."**

It is similar for us as well. When we undertake a task, its outcome is already in motion toward us. The uncertainty lies in how and when this outcome will manifest. If only we had a way to track the real-time progress of the fruits of our actions, we too could feel assured and content, knowing that the results are on their way and will surely reach us in due course!

Unfortunately, nature does not provide live updates on the results of our actions! Instead, it encourages us to pray, have faith, and trust its unwavering laws. If we have taken certain actions, corresponding results are inevitable. We should wait for these results patiently and joyfully. Those who can do this find contentment through patience.

**Points for contemplation**

1. Reflect on how you feel and behave during the period between taking action and awaiting results. Do you find yourself restless, or are you able to practice patience?

2. Reflect on an experience where, upon receiving certain results, you thought, "I unnecessarily worried and stressed over the outcome. I could have spent that time in peace and happiness instead."

3. If you are presently waiting for the outcome of your efforts, examine your mental state during this waiting period. Are you waiting with impatience or with the feeling of "Wait, watch with wonder"? Remember the laws of nature and tell yourself, "I trust nature completely. Everything happens in my life at the right time and in the right way."

**Case study**

Vikram and Betaal's story is a well-known Indian folklore. Vikram represents wisdom, while Betaal represents doubts. If Betaal were to ask Vikram, "Just as tracking the cab reassured the mother about her son, can God give His devotees real-time updates too? If so, how would He do it? O King Vikram, please answer my question." What would Vikram say in response to Betaal?

# 16
# The Address of Contentment

In an Indian mythological story, an ascetic was wandering in a jungle when he met Sage Narada. The sage asked him, "What are you doing in this dense jungle, my child? The wild animals in this jungle might attack you." The ascetic fell at Sage Narada's feet and begged him, "I have earned much in life, gained everything –wealth, fame, social respect, good relations, and a loving son and daughter-in-law, but I am still not content. I roamed the world in search of contentment. Finally, a sage told me, 'You won't find contentment in this material world of short-lived pleasures.' Hearing this, I renounced the world and have been roaming around in the jungles since then. I have been seeking contentment for years, but have not found it anywhere."

Sage Narada replied, "I deeply empathize with you, my dear child. Hence, I will tell you the address of contentment today." Hearing this, the ascetic's face lit up with joy. He asked, "O revered sage, please tell me where contentment resides."

The sage revealed the secret, "Contentment is neither in the past nor in the future, neither in the world nor away from it, neither in gaining something nor in losing something. Contentment resides in the present moment. It is right here, right now, within you. You don't need to search for it anywhere else. Just come out of this feeling that you are not content and that you must find something to be contented."

When we search for something, it implies we consider it missing. For instance, when we lose something, we search for it. When we set a goal, we strive to pursue it. By pursuing, we attain it. Thus, by searching, we regain what was lost, but contentment cannot be found by searching. We can feel contentment only when we understand the truth and stop searching.

We have associated contentment with other things. For example, "If this happens, I would be contented. If this does not happen, I cannot be contented." When things do not turn out like that, we feel contentment is missing and start searching for it. Instead, if we start believing that **"Whatever I have, in whichever condition I am, and wherever I am at present, is the best. I am completely content here and now,"** then this is true contentment.

Contentment does not come and go. It is always present within us. But we fail to always feel it. The solution is to eliminate the reasons why we don't feel it so that we can experience true contentment.

True contentment resides in the present moment. Hence, to experience it, we must also bring ourselves to the present and remain in the now. However, people find this very challenging. They just cannot remain in the present. They are either lost in their memories or busy imagining their future. If they are not lost in both, they are lost in social media or other forms of entertainment.

Even while working, they remain completely available in the present for very few moments. Most of the time, their minds are occupied either with memories related to the work done in the past or thoughts about the future consequences of the work.

If we carefully observe, in twenty-four hours, people hardly spend a few minutes mindfully in the present; the rest of the time is spent in non-awareness.

The more they stay away from the present, the more their minds indulge in unnecessary acrobatics. They look around themselves and form false beliefs that they lack many things that others have. And the game of discontentment continues. But if they remain in the present, their minds won't find an opportunity to indulge in acrobatics at all.

> **Is whatever you seek leading you toward contentment? If the direction is right, every step will lead you closer to your goal. If the direction is wrong, the more you run, the farther you move away from your goal.**

**How to stay in the present**

To stay in the present, we must learn the art of seeing the present. Let us understand how to see the present with an example.

Ramesh was going to the park for his morning walk when he saw one of his acquaintances walking. At that moment, Ramesh was just seeing that person. Now, there are two possibilities for this act of seeing.

The first one is—Ramesh saw the person, wished him "Good morning," and continued walking. He did not think about that person anymore.

The second possibility is—Ramesh saw the person and continued walking ahead. However, on the way, thoughts about that person arose within him. "Oh, he seems to have lost weight. Maybe he walks more. I just cannot walk so much. The last time I tried to walk more, my blood pressure increased, and I had to visit the doctor. I had to take leave from work for that. My boss was so angry with me. This company is pathetic. I just can't take a day off. I feel like quitting this job, but I'm not getting a job elsewhere. I have given an interview in the other company but I'm not sure when I'll get to know the outcome. Even if I do get that job, what if I am deputed to another city? What will I do then? There are still six months left for the children to finish their term in school. If I have to join immediately, I will have to go alone. How will my wife manage the children alone?"

In this way, even if Ramesh was physically walking in the present, his mind was lost in acrobatics between the past and the future. If we observe closely, it was such a trivial incident—Ramesh met the acquaintance and wished him, "Good morning." He could have just moved ahead after wishing him and observed the next scene by being in the present. But it doesn't happen. The mind just needs a pretext to start its needless somersaults and create a web of illusory thoughts by looking at one scene. Ramesh had gone for a morning walk to keep himself healthy and peaceful, but he returned with a lot of worries instead.

Our mind refuses to stay in the present. It is restless by nature. We must consciously train it, much like a wild horse. When the mind begins to jump from the present moment to the past or future, immediately stop it. Instruct it to remain in the now.

Imagine if Ramesh had acted according to the first possibility, what would have happened? He would have wished his acquaintance "Good morning" and moved ahead. Later on, while walking ahead, he would have noticed the beautiful variety of flowers, plants, and birds. He would have observed them and moved ahead. He would have remained in the present during his entire walk and returned home happy and peaceful.

Several meditation techniques have been devised to train our restless mind to remain in the present most of the time. For example, thought numbering, breath-watching, and so on. In thought numbering meditation, we watch our thoughts and number them. In breath-watching meditation, we witness the incoming and outgoing breath.

In this way, when the mind learns to consciously remain in the present for some time in meditation, the same state can continue even while walking. But for that, you must start practicing meditation consistently. Those who meditate regularly are more peaceful, stable, and content compared to others because they have trained their minds to remain in the present.

**Points for contemplation**

1   Reflect on the last 10 minutes and see how long you remained in the present. For how long did your mind drift away from the present to the past or future?

2   Whenever you feel discontented, try to keep your mind focused on the present moment for some time. Observe whether this changes your feeling of discontentment.

3   For some days, regularly practice meditations to remain in the present. Then continue this practice even while walking.

---

**Case study**

Imagine, in the story of Vikram and Betaal, just like you, Vikram works on all the case studies in this book. Betaal becomes distressed and scared seeing Vikram's progress. He is scared that once Vikram learns the secret, Betaal will have no option but to leave his life. What secret have you learned in this chapter because of which Betaal (the embodiment of doubts) will be forced to leave?

# 17
# When the Mind and Work Are Not in Tandem

It was the first day of Diwali. As soon as Sanjana opened her eyes in the morning, all the tasks she had to do throughout the day flashed before her eyes. A nagging thought arose within her, "Why do these festivals come?" She started feeling anxious and distressed.

Gradually, this one negative thought completely engulfed her. Then, the barrage of thoughts began: "So many extra tasks ranging from cleaning to shopping come up during festivals. There is so much to consider for everyone—from guests to helpers, children to adults, family to neighbors—what to buy for everyone, whom to invite when, and when to visit others. Oh dear... the list is endless!"

Besides these extra tasks, daily activities at home and office also needed to be completed. It is said that festivals are meant to fill our lives with happiness and enthusiasm. But for Sanjana, it was just the opposite. She felt as though festivals made her life more stressful and worrying. She started praying, "Let the day somehow pass so I can be peaceful and content once again."

Many people experience similar feelings as Sanjana did. They feel burdened by the arrival of festivals or celebration of some special occasions.

As Sanjana's mind was clouded with so many thoughts, she was mentally upset, and her irritation was reflected in her speech as well. She had to clean and decorate the house, draw *Rangoli* (a form of Indian art that is drawn at the entrance of the house), and then go to the market for shopping. During Diwali days, the markets were so crowded that just thinking about navigating through the crowd stressed her. She started thinking, "Why do we need to celebrate Diwali in this way only? In this hustle and bustle, the festival's true meaning and joy are lost. It feels like a race. Why doesn't anyone take a pause and think if this festival can also be celebrated with ease and happiness?"

Sanjana felt a sense of discontentment within herself. There were so many activities that she started with one and didn't realize when she shifted to the next one, leaving the first one incomplete. In between, continuous phone calls from her well-wishers disturbed her even more. She felt like leaving everything and going somewhere else to sit in peace. Amid this chaos, a prayer arose in her mind, **"O God, let me remember the right teachings at the right time. May I receive the right guidance. Thank you so much for giving me the right thoughts."**

As a result of the right prayer offered at the right time, Sanjana's negative thoughts began to subside. Now, a thought arose in her mind that compelled her to contemplate: "After all, why am I feeling so distressed? Is life really so tough? Do festivals truly cause so much hardship?" In response, gradually, subtle reminders came to light, and she started contemplating in that direction.

She pondered on the very first thought that had started her train of negative thoughts and realized that she must regard her thoughts like children. Just like parents apply a soothing balm to the wounds of children without scolding them, we must also apply the balm of love, joy, peace, amazement, and goodwill to our negative feelings.

Whenever thoughts trouble, apply the balm of self-enquiry to these wounded thoughts. Also, check what is truly missing here. You will realize that nothing is missing except you! You feel something is missing because you are running away into the future without rejoicing in the present moment. You are running the blind race by following the herd instinct.

You have deviated from your true nature in an attempt to please others. Therefore, you are far away from experiencing contentment.

Whenever you feel there is more work, ask yourself, "Is the work really more, or is the thought more powerful, which is sneaking into my contentment?"

Let us understand this with another example. What would you tell a person who is wearing his spectacles on his head but searching for them everywhere else? You will say, "Stop searching. The spectacles are on your head." Similarly, contentment is very much within you in the present, but you search for it everywhere else, in the past and the future.

During festivals, when you feel you have to spend so much time and money on shopping, ask yourself, "What has more value—the clothes or the children for whom I am shopping?" You would receive the answer that clothes do not have much value, but your children are priceless! Then you will happily go shopping and also pray, "**Let there be such arrangements that next time, the festival can be celebrated in an even better manner.**"

Therefore, it is up to you whether to remain unhappy by rejecting the festival or rejoice in it by accepting it. Acceptance brings happiness, freedom, and contentment. For example, if a thorn pricks you, what would you do? You would work sensibly to remove the thorn first and then proceed with your work. Similarly, in every incident of life, first remove the thorn of discontentment and then proceed with your work.

---

> Behind every desire lies the true desire for contentment. Then why not start with contentment itself? This is indeed possible; experience it with the practice of true meditation.

---

Here are some points that can help you feel peaceful and contented in various situations.

**Stop overthinking**

Whatever the circumstances, do not label them as good or bad. Accept them as they are. When you do not accept them, it builds resistance within and gives rise to needless thoughts.

**Do not let your energy go down**

While doing any work, completely focus on it without thinking of any other tasks. For instance, if you have gone shopping, fully focus on it. If you start thinking about pending activities at home or in the office while shopping, you will feel impatient and discontented. Whenever your mind tends to wander, tell yourself, **"Let me completely focus on the work I am doing right now."**

When you jump from the present moment to the past or the future, it disturbs your present task and lowers your energy. Therefore, fully focus on the task at hand and completely remain in the present.

**Prioritize your work**

Under certain special circumstances like festivals, functions at home, or while going out somewhere, additional tasks come up, increasing the workload. At such times, first and foremost, prioritize your activities. Routine activities happen daily. Office work also continues. Remind yourself that this special time is for special tasks. You must make yourself available for these special tasks. Prioritize which activities should be done first, which can be done later, and how much time should be allocated for each activity.

If some activities can be done beforehand or postponed for later, prioritize and act on them accordingly. For example, most people clean up their homes a week before Diwali. It can be done a little earlier, too. You can even shop the things you need for Diwali in advance. Similarly, plan your office work in a way that you have extra time for special occasions.

**Do not seek perfection**

Always remember that there is no such thing as perfection. Hence, do not seek perfection in the things you do. Work to the best of your ability. Then whatever you accomplish, however it turns out, that is its perfect state. If you compare your work with others, you will feel distressed.

For example, Sanjana drew a beautiful Rangoli outside her home. But when she saw her neighbor's Rangoli, she felt hers was not up to the mark. So, she spent a couple of hours perfecting her Rangoli which delayed her other household tasks. Then she felt irritated. In this way, neither did she feel contented in drawing the Rangoli nor doing her pending household tasks. Then she started lamenting, "After all, why do these festivals come?"

Therefore, do not get stuck seeking perfection, do not compare your work with others, accomplish your work with joy, and seek contentment within the work itself.

**Consider tough circumstances as a game**

When we get attached to any situation and want things to happen our way, we tend to lose our peace, happiness, and contentment. In such times, bring yourself into a witnessing mode. Tell yourself, "I will only witness this situation. Whatever happens, however it happens, is in the hands of God. I surrender to God and witness my body acting by His guidance."

In this way, when you give up your doer-ship and observe situations with a witness attitude, even the toughest of circumstances will seem like a game to you. For example, if you get attached to a specific team in a cricket match, you go through an emotional upheaval during the entire match. If the team performs well, you feel elated. Otherwise, you feel dejected about their poor performance. Some fans become so hysterical that they even break their TV sets. Some cannot endure it and even experience heart attacks. However, if you are not attached to any specific team, you enjoy watching the game of both teams. Then, you cheer at every shot and genuinely appreciate the game, which is the true purpose of the sport.

We must also play similarly in life situations. We must live life with the right sporting spirit without getting attached to anything. In this way, you can face even adverse circumstances with happiness and contentment.

**Points for contemplation**

1. Does your mind wander elsewhere while you are working on something? If yes, reflect on the losses you have incurred or can potentially face because of that. Write them down.
2. Do you plan for special occasions (festivals, weddings, parties, etc.) beforehand or wait until the last minute?

---

**Case study**

One day, your sister bangs on your door loudly, waking you up. She seems to be going about all the housework in agitation. Her negative vibrations spoil the atmosphere at home. Some guests are visiting to meet her for a marriage alliance in the evening. Contemplate and write down how you will calm her down and change the atmosphere at home.

# 18
# The Feeling of Completeness

When you want to say something to someone but cannot, you feel disturbed and discontented. Once you communicate clearly and fully, you feel complete and content. If your work is pending, you feel disturbed. You experience completeness once the work is done.

If you receive something that does not make you feel complete, even if it is complete in itself, you still experience a sense of incompleteness. For instance, a mother has two children but only one laddoo (an Indian sweet). She breaks the laddoo into halves and gives each child a half. Both children feel they have not received a complete laddoo. The mother then takes both the halves, rolls them into two smaller laddoos, and gives them back to her children. Now, both children feel happy and complete with their mini-laddoos!

When you are given half a laddoo, you are reminded of the missing half and feel incomplete. However, when both halves are reshaped into smaller, whole laddoos, you feel complete upon receiving them, even if they are smaller. When there is no sense of lack, there is a feeling of completeness. This feeling of completeness brings us closer to true contentment.

**What is the feeling of completeness?**

Everything is complete in itself. But if we see something as incomplete, it may be because our beliefs are blocking us from seeing its completeness.

For example, a person watched a film in which the hero and heroine were separated despite loving each other and never reunited. Each went on with their own lives. After he finished watching the film and left the theater, he said, "What a bad film! The director didn't give it a proper ending."

When asked why he felt the film lacked a proper ending, he replied, "The hero and heroine should have been reunited." From the many films he had watched since childhood, he developed a firm belief that the hero and heroine must always be reunited at the end; otherwise, the story is incomplete. This belief left him discontented after watching the film.

Similarly, many people often hold beliefs that prevent them from experiencing true contentment, making them feel incomplete. They also hold onto many grievances, retorts, and words they plan to say someday. Until they express them, they remain in a state of discontentment.

An old man had dreamed of traveling by air since childhood, but he never got the chance to fulfill this dream. Despite achieving everything else in life, this unfulfilled desire haunted him until the end. This is similar to people who intend to go on pilgrimages but cannot, and feel that their lives are incomplete without it. Many people harbor unfulfilled desires, leading them to live with a sense of incompleteness.

For some people, not fulfilling major desires causes discontent, while for others, even minor desires can lead to discontentment. For instance, someone who is unable to eat their favorite dish for a month may feel discontented throughout that time. Thus, petty desires can also trigger feelings of discontentment in people.

### Feeling of incompleteness on the path to seeking the truth of life

A sorrowful and troubled seventy-year-old man once met a spiritual guru and confided, "I have been meditating diligently for the past thirty years. I have shunned sin and negativity and have been leading a disciplined Satvik lifestyle dedicated to the pursuit of the ultimate truth. However, I have never experienced anything profound in my practice of meditation. Now, I feel I've wasted the last thirty years."

The guru asked him, "Do you meditate with the expectation of experiencing something extraordinary, like feeling weightless, recalling past lives, glimpsing a specific deity, or seeing bright lights?"

The man replied, "Not necessarily those specific experiences, but I expected to feel something that would show that my meditation was worthwhile."

The guru replied, "This expectation has hindered your meditation from becoming successful. How can your meditation be successful when you are bogged down by the expectation for a specific experience? The purpose of meditation is to be a detached witness and simply observe whatever arises in your awareness. Without proper guidance, your own beliefs and expectations of meditation have trapped you in discontentment and incompleteness."

---

**When all work is done joyfully without stress, one experiences true contentment while also achieving worldly success.**

---

### Discontentment due to pending work

Some people habitually plan their work and insist on completing it within a set time frame. When this does not happen, they feel incomplete. Even if the work can be done later without any consequence, they struggle to accept it. Instead, they become impatient and wonder why they cannot meet their deadlines, which makes them feel incomplete.

The root cause of this feeling of incompleteness lies in our beliefs and our definition of completeness. We think we can only feel complete when things go a certain way.

But we should view this from a different angle. From the time we are born, some work is always ongoing. When one task finishes, another begins, or multiple tasks continue simultaneously. Activity is the expression of life. Therefore, the amount of work completed within a given time is exactly as much as it should be. Our belief that more work should have been done within a specified time period stems from our conditioning.

Let us release all feelings of incompleteness we have held onto and embrace the feeling of completeness. Let us tell ourselves, **"At this moment, whatever work is done is complete in itself. I am complete. In this feeling of completeness, all my work is finishing on time. Whatever was necessary for today is completed."**

Let us increase our alignment with nature. If we need to say something to someone or do something, nature will provide opportunities. We must make the best use of these opportunities by acting at the right time. Until then, let us not waste our time feeling incomplete.

### Completion of pending work

Some people are able to complete work on time but choose not to. They hide their incompetency or laziness under the mask of fake contentment to avoid tasks or delegate them to others. Despite this façade, they remain discontented within. They may fool others but cannot fool themselves or Nature.

If we have given our full effort and some work remains pending, we should consider it complete for that time period and embrace the feeling of completeness. If there is pending work that we can complete, we should avoid hesitation or procrastination and finish it.

### Points for contemplation

1. Take a moment to contemplate the areas in your life where you carry the burden of incompleteness. How much discontent are you feeling because of this?

2. Release these feelings of incompleteness by telling yourself, "This incompleteness was an incorrect belief that I had assumed as the truth. Whatever the state right now, it is complete exactly as it is. Any more work that needs to be completed, will be completed at its right time."
3. If there is any pending work you can complete but haven't due to your latent patterns like laziness, complaints, hesitation, or procrastination, acknowledge this and finish the work within the necessary time.

---

**Case study**

If Betaal were to ask Vikram another question, "O King, how often have you felt complete in the spiritual, social, financial, mental, and physical aspects of your life?" If you were Vikram, what would be your reply for all the five facets of life?

# 19
# Contentment at Work

The work we do, especially for our livelihood, is deeply related to our sense of contentment. However, very few people experience contentment in their work. What is that factor which leads to experiencing contentment at work? Is it progress at work, creativity, money, desired outcome, quality of work, recognition gained from the work, praise, or something else? Let us understand this with an example.

A furniture factory owner wanted to know whether his employees find more contentment in the process of working or in the money they earn from it.

His manager said, "I will practically demonstrate the answer to you." The manager went to a place in the jungle where one of their workers was cutting a tree with an axe to make furniture. The manager asked the worker, "How long do you take to cut down a tree?" The worker replied, "Half a day." The manager asked, "How much do you earn for this work?" The worker replied, "Rs. 300 for a tree." The manager told him, "I will pay you Rs. 3000 for cutting down a tree, but the condition is that you will use a hammer instead of an axe."

The worker thought to himself, "Whether I use an axe or a hammer, I have to cut down a tree. Although it will take more effort with a hammer, I will also earn ten times more money." He agreed.

The next day, he started striking the tree with a hammer. He spent the entire day striking it but could manage to cut only a part of the tree with great difficulty. He took four days to cut down the entire tree with the hammer. During this time, he would have cut eight trees with an axe and earned Rs. 2400. Now, he was earning Rs. 3000 for cutting down just one tree using a hammer.

In terms of money, the deal was profitable, but was he content with his work? Did he work with the same ease and joy as he used to while cutting down trees with an axe? Now, he also had to cut down the next tree with a hammer. He wondered whether he should take up the next task.

Like the worker, many people are caught up in this dilemma: Should they seek contentment in the work they do or the money they earn?

**What is more important?**

These days, people prioritize money over everything else. In the pursuit of earning more money, they end up doing work that they never wanted to do throughout their lives. They certainly make good money but do not experience contentment and happiness from their work. Instead, they undergo a lot of stress, struggle, and negativity, which badly affects their mental and physical health. Working in this manner, becomes a painful burden without any joy.

Many people spend most of their time at work. If they do not find happiness and contentment in their work, they spend the remaining time in sorrow and discontentment. Even if they earn a lot, what is the value of living such a life? Instead, it is far more valuable if they earn a little less money with contentment and happiness.

Everyone can have different opinions about this. Some may justify that earning more money is more important. But it is also true that as our income increases, our expenses also increase proportionately. We tend to spend more on extra clothes and gadgets or make travel plans.

Thus, our necessities change based on our income. As the income increases, so do our necessities. Given this, no matter how much more we earn, it can never make us feel contented. Therefore, those who want peace, joy, and contentment in their life should never associate these values with money. They should work to establish the right balance between the money earned and the job satisfaction derived. Their emphasis is more on job satisfaction.

Now, let us come back to the story of the worker at the furniture factory. He refused to cut down the next tree with the hammer. He said, "I already know a better way of cutting down trees, then why should I use a hammer? I don't feel contented cutting trees with a hammer, even I am paid more. I will only use an axe. I will find some creative ways to cut them in a shorter time. My work will finish faster and in a better manner."

Those who solely work for money can be considered working with a hammer. They need to reflect on the areas of life where they are using a hammer instead of an axe. This means, they need to contemplate whether they are doing wrong work or doing work in the wrong way in an attempt to earn more money. Are they following wrong practices? Are they being deceitful at work? If they use a hammer, they will get money but will not feel contented. They will always experience a sense of lack. Then, a day will come when they will think of leaving everything and running away.

Saint Kabir was a weaver. He used to work from morning till night and then meditate on God. Saint Ravidas was a cobbler. He used to make shoes the whole day, singing songs in praise of God. They were content with the work they did. They did not focus on how much they were earning. They also managed their households with the money they earned.

Therefore, ask yourself, "What is important in your life: money or contentment, flaunting or happiness, convenience or peace?" Based on this assessment, make your decision.

---

**If your energies are scattered, you will experience sorrow and discontentment. If you are attracted to feelings of divine devotion and resolve, there will be a quest to attain the truth.**

**The mantra for contentment at work**

Contentment at work comes with creativity, while contentment with the outcome of work comes from detachment.

When we continue to do any work in the same manner, it becomes a mechanical ritual, which eventually leads to boredom. We begin to find the work less interesting, and we wish to change the activity. Then, we start looking for this change outside by changing our jobs, our city of residence, or our role at work.

However, if we bring creativity into the way we work and start doing it differently, we won't need to change anything outside.

Creativity means working in a better way, differently, in less time, and learning something new in the spare time. It can make yourself and others feel contented. For example, a master chef makes subtle changes to the same dish and presents it differently. This brings novelty and joy to both the chef and those who eat it. In other words, creativity is the quality that brings contentment and happiness at work, accomplishing work in a better manner.

However, many people struggle to bring creativity into their work because they are not concerned about how the work is done. They just want to finish their work and earn money. They are more concerned and attached to the outcome of their action. They somehow complete their work mechanically, with a sense of boredom, and remain discontented. As a result, they do not achieve the desired outcome and continue to remain discontented. Most people compromise the quality of their work if they are paid less. They complete their work in less time in a careless manner, even if it does not give them satisfaction.

Only those who accomplish their work honestly, creatively, skillfully, and efficiently experience true contentment through their work. The rest experience discontentment both while doing their work and after completing it. On the contrary, if we perform the work creatively and remain detached from its outcome, we will feel contented while doing the work as well as after receiving its outcome.

There was a famous painter who worked for a month and made a beautiful painting. When a connoisseur of art saw the painting, he exclaimed in amazement, "Wow! What a masterpiece you have created. You will get at least one crore rupees for this painting. You must have toiled hard to create it."

The painter replied with a smile, "I didn't create this painting with hard work but with joy. I experienced so much joy and contentment that I felt my life became fulfilled just by creating it. I didn't feel attached to how much money it would fetch. Whether it would be sold or not makes no difference to me."

Just like this painter, **those who focus on creativity are not attached to the outcome, and those who focus on the outcome cannot grasp the depth of creativity.** Further, those who are not creative at work can never find contentment in it. Therefore, it is said that if you want to experience contentment in life, bring creativity to your work and remain detached from its outcome.

**Points for contemplation**

1. Reflect on the work you do for your livelihood and observe with what sentiment you perform it. How do you feel while working? Are you content with your work or feel bored and want a change?

2. Reflect on the work you perform daily at your home or office. Did you do it in the same manner yesterday as you have been for many days, or is there an element of creativity in it?

3. Reflect on the work you do for your livelihood to examine whether your focus is more on doing good work in a better way or the money earned from it. If you were paid less for that work, would you compromise on the quality of your work? If yes, then contemplate the reasons behind it.

### Case study

Betaal now asks Vikram, "O King, the epic Ramayana is renowned in Indian tradition. It features a mention of Hanuman, who is an inspiration for the new generation. Now, answer my question: With what sentiment and attitude did Hanuman work? What do you learn from Hanuman's deeds in the Ramayana?

## 20
## Towards Supreme Contentment

Once, a household faced an unusual problem: The bulbs would intermittently light up and go off. Frustrated, the owner replaced all the bulbs, but the issue persisted. A neighbor suggested checking the house's electrical wiring. Despite inspecting the bulb holders and wiring, he found nothing amiss. The owner eventually called an electrician for help.

The electrician checked and told him that replacing the bulbs and inspecting the holders and wiring was an utter waste of time and money. The actual issue lay with the main electric supply point. Once this was fixed, all the bulbs in the house started working properly.

In a similar vein, an aged man suffered from ill health, experiencing headaches, high blood pressure, high cholesterol, and skin allergies. Consequently, he had to take many medicines. One day, he consulted a doctor in a different city. After examining him, the doctor concluded that he had only one problem: a stomach infection. This infection was the root cause of his other ailments, which were merely symptoms. Once the infection was treated, all his other ailments disappeared.

Similarly, we often see many problems in our lives that keep us discontented, such as unfulfilled desires, worries about the future, a sense of lack, fear, impatience, restlessness, distraction, and hopelessness. We must realize that these are merely symptoms of an underlying issue within us. If we address the root cause, all these problems will disappear.

In a house of cards game, when the card at the foundation is removed, the whole house comes tumbling down. Similarly, if we eliminate the root cause of our problems, they will all disappear. We would then experience abundance and supreme contentment. This contentment would not depend on the presence or absence of anything in our lives. It would be an independent feeling, regardless of our circumstances.

### Devotion backed by wisdom: The solution to the root cause

One common trait among truly content people is their complete surrender to the divine will. When devotion is blind, it cannot sustain true contentment. Without knowledge, some discontentment always lingers. Blind devotion to God often comes with expectations and beliefs about the afterlife, heaven and hell, good and evil. True contentment arises from divine devotion that is grounded in wisdom. **Devotion backed by wisdom is the key to supreme contentment.**

Wrong beliefs cause discontentment. At the root of all wrong beliefs is the fundamental belief that we are separate individuals, defined by the personality we assume. By challenging this sense of separate individuality, we can dissolve this false identity and eliminate the root cause of all discontentment.

Eliminating individuality does not mean harming ourselves. It means removing the belief that separates us from our Source, from God. This belief makes us think we are distinct entities defined by our body-mind. We can put an end to this belief with the sword of wisdom-based devotion. Many saints, like Kabir, Ravidas, Tulsidas, Soordas, and Tukaram, have transcended their ego-based identities and experienced supreme contentment.

Before we delve deeper into this subject, we must realize who we truly are. Who are we who consider ourselves separate entities and lead lives of discontentment?

**Who am I that is discontented?**

The answer to this question is found within the question itself—it is the "I." The sense of a distinct "I" is the root cause of discontentment. Let us explore this with an analogy to understand what this sense of "I" truly is.

When a wave rises in the ocean, it begins to believe it has a separate existence, distinct from the ocean. It starts feeling the sense of "I" and perceives itself as separate from the ocean. When it sees other waves, it believes they are all different from it. But when this wave gains wisdom and devotion, it realizes it has risen from the ocean and is merely a part of it. The feeling of "I" disappears, and it experiences true contentment in merging back into the ocean.

We are all parts of the same Whole, known by many names, such as Supreme Consciousness, the Universe, the Higher Self, the Source, God, Ishwar, Allah, Christ, and more. To simplify, we will use the word "Self" to refer to this Whole, as it is the common essence of all religions.

Everything we think or feel originates from the Self, which exists within and around our body-mind.

When a child is born, it is one with the Self. It does not have a separate identity and the sense of a distinct "I." All actions occur through the intuitive mind in the child, which is guided by the Self. The intuitive mind is an expression of the Self. The Self lives, experiences, and expresses itself through our body-mind. There is no other separate entity apart from the Self.

However, as we grow and observe others, we gradually develop an individual identity that separates us from the Self. We start to believe in our independence as unique individuals, distinct from others.

This separate "I" is essentially a myth—merely a thought that becomes so powerful that it shapes our entire lives. We mistakenly identify ourselves solely with our body-mind. We believe in an existence separate from the Self that encompasses everyone else.

The illusion of this false "I" keeps us disconnected from our true identity as the Self. When this sense of individuality solidifies during childhood, we unknowingly distance ourselves from God, inviting all the troubles in our lives.

We can liken the relationship between man and God to a modern technology example. Imagine a large company with a powerful main server. Numerous computer terminals worldwide connect to this server. Each terminal only has a display screen and a keyboard. All processing happens on the main server. However, to the operator working on a terminal, it appears the terminal is functioning independently, unaware that the main server is doing all the work behind the scenes.

Drawing parallels to this example, we are like computer terminals that mistakenly believe, "I am independent, and I do all my work." This misconception arises from our ignorance. The truth is that everything originates from the Self, unfolds in the Self, is driven by the Self, and serves the Self. There is no separate "I."

To dispel this ignorance, wise seers have expounded various spiritual paths, such as *Bhakti yoga* (path of devotion), *Gyan yoga* (path of wisdom), and *Karma yoga* (path of righteous deeds). These paths guide us toward the realization that we are not individual terminals; rather, everything unfolds because of the main server—the Self.

---

**When engaged in creative pursuits, if you feel both joy and contentment, recognize that this is the work you are meant to do in your life on Earth.**

---

### Knowledge removes the sense of doer-ship

Yogesh went to the mall and parked his new car. After shopping, he returned to the parking lot to find the car had been bumped, leaving a deep dent and scratches on the bumper. Frustrated and upset, he began shouting at the parking attendant.

Just then, Nilesh arrived at the parking lot and also began shouting, "My car, which I bought just a few days ago, has been damaged today. I won't let the culprit get away with this."

Upon closer inspection of the number-plate, Yogesh realized that it wasn't his car that had been damaged. Feeling greatly relieved, he turned to Nilesh and reassured him, "Please don't worry. Your car is new and covered by warranty and insurance. The repairs will be taken care of by the insurance company."

Yogesh gave Nilesh the right advice, but he could only do so after realizing that the damaged car was not his own.

So, what do we understand from this story?

In essence, when we feel the sense of "I" or "mine," we become entangled in thoughts like, "This is mine," "That is not mine," "This should not happen to me," etc. Our attachment to our life stories, bodies, and possessions causes disturbance when things go wrong, clouding our inner clarity. However, when similar issues affect others, we can easily advise them on what is right and wrong without personal distress.

When our own child fails an exam, we often feel disturbed and may scold them. However, when a neighbor's child fails, we readily console them, saying things like, "It's okay. Exams come every year. Your child can study hard and do better next time. It's just an exam!"

If we cultivate detachment from our possessions, relationships, bodies, thoughts, emotions, and external circumstances, we can think more clearly and objectively for ourselves, similar to how we advise others.

When we encounter losses, we can remind ourselves, "It's okay. Gain and loss are natural in life. There is much more to gain. The car may be dented, but this incident cannot dent my spirit!"

Detachment becomes possible when we stop identifying with our body-mind and recognize our inherent oneness with the Self. It is the Self that directs both our actions and our lives. The right thoughts and actions for us emerge naturally from the Self, precisely when needed. This alignment ensures not just contentment but a profound sense of supreme contentment.

**Points for contemplation**

1. Consider something in your life that currently makes you sad or that you feel is lacking. If a friend or someone you know were experiencing the same thing, what advice would you offer them?
2. Reflect on whether the advice you would offer others in a given situation is something you could apply to yourself. If you find it challenging to follow your own advice, what is the reason? Introspect what you assume yourself to be.

---

**Case study**

In the Indian epic, the Mahabharata, the Pandava prince Arjuna initially hesitated to fight his relatives in the battle of Kurukshetra. However, after receiving wisdom and guidance from Lord Krishna, Arjuna's perspective shifted, and he became ready and willing to engage in the war. On the other hand, Duryodhana, the Kaurava prince, was too arrogant to heed any advice. He insisted on going to war.

If you could advise Duryodhana, based on the discussions in this chapter, what would you tell him?

## 21
## The Perspective for Contentment

A journalist traveled to the hills to film a documentary about a temple's construction. He saw laborers breaking stones and approached one of them. "Brother, how long have you been working here? How are you feeling? Are you facing any difficulties?" he asked.

The laborer was irritated and retorted, "Can't you see what I'm doing? I'm breaking stones in this heat with blisters on my hands. This is my fate! A temple is being built where God will reside. People will come to seek blessings, and He will grant their wishes. But look at me! Toiling in this sweltering heat for meager wages is my fate."

The journalist consoled him and moved on. He approached the next laborer and asked the same question. The laborer paused and quietly replied, "Every job has its problems. But this work provides for my family. Breaking stones earns me daily wages to support my wife, children, and parents."

The journalist noticed that this laborer was quite content with his job. He found satisfaction in earning money to support his family.

The journalist moved on to a third laborer, who was humming a *bhajan* (devotional song) as he worked. The journalist noticed a twinkle in his eyes, a sparkle often seen when someone achieves something grand.

When the journalist asked him the same question, the man paused and smiled warmly. "I feel honored and blessed to be a part of building this temple for the Almighty," he replied. "My sweat is blessed as it falls where the Lord will reside. Just thinking about it fills me with happiness!"

The journalist wondered, "It's strange that the circumstances are the same for all the laborers: the same hill, the same heat, the same spade and hammer, the same task, and the same blisters. Yet, one laborer complains bitterly, another is content with his duty, and the third is blissful and fully content."

What causes the difference in their behaviors? The circumstances are the same, but their perspective and attitude make all the difference. One sees his job as a burden, the second views it as a responsibility, and the third embraces it as an opportunity for divine service.

---

**The key to a happy and fulfilled life is to connect and align with the Source and follow its guidance in everything we do.**

---

Let us understand the key takeaways from the above story.

Our happiness at work depends on how we perceive it. True contentment comes from seeing our work as a form of service, regardless of what work we do. Instead of seeing work as a burden, consider it a service to God. When we approach our work as a way to serve God, we find joy and supreme contentment.

Every profession or career should be seen as a means of serving God, going beyond our own needs. We should feel thankful and honored that God has entrusted us with the opportunity to help others. This not only brings happiness and contentment but also enhances the quality of our work.

No matter what work we do, cherish it as a divine opportunity and a blessing. Regardless of the comforts and possessions at our disposal, we should offer our efforts with the attitude of service. Happiness naturally arises when we work with this attitude, elevating our way of life. By working from a place of contentment rather than striving for it, we achieve a higher state of being.

To live happily, we should learn from challenges, regarding each difficulty as a valuable lesson. While persevering through difficulties, we must prioritize maintaining our inner contentment.

**Points for contemplation**

1. Are you fully content with your work? If so, why? If not, what's the reason?
2. Which laborer's perspective inspires you the most and why?
3. What attitude do you think leads to lasting happiness and contentment?
4. How do you plan to use what you've learned from this chapter in your life?

---

**Case study**

Neeta, a senior engineer at a multinational software company, has been offered a prestigious assignment in the company's US office due to her talent and performance. Despite her family's excitement, Neeta's heart is set on staying in her own country to contribute to its progress. Now, she faces pressure from her family and the company to accept the American offer.

What would you advise Neeta and her family? What matters most to her—money, family, or her happiness? Which choice would bring her the most contentment?

## 22
## Principles for Complete Contentment

There are some key principles to lead a fully contented life. If one incorporates them into their life, they can never feel discontented. Let us understand five of them and try to implement them in our lives.

**Principle 1: Avoid being your own master; be at the service of God**

If a company earns profits, its owner is the happiest, and when it suffers losses, the owner experiences the most sorrow. The ups and downs in the company's performance cause ups and downs in the owner's life. They always continue to think of ways to generate more revenue and maximize profit. Caught up in the desire for more, the owner never feels contented.

However, the lives of the employees remain unaffected by the ups and downs faced by the company. Whether the company earns more profit or less, they continue to perform their duties and receive their salaries at the end of the month.

Similarly, we must learn to lead our lives not by being our own master but by serving. But whom should we serve? We must make God the owner and leave the reins of our lives in His hands. We must surrender our lives to Him.

Whatever good or bad happens in life, whatever is gained or lost, we must entrust it to God. Tell God, "I surrender my life to you. I will do my work with honesty and hard work. After that, I will accept whatever I receive as my salary from you and happily live with it."

With this attitude, you will feel contented in all situations. No external ups and downs can affect you.

## Principle 2: Everything belongs to God

The biggest cause of discontentment is things not happening according to our will. We always want to see things happening exactly as we wish, but things happen according to God's will. Hence, always remain in this feeling, "O God, whatever I possess, what I believe to be mine, is all Yours. My happiness and sorrow, success and failure, close and distant relationships, desires and disappointments, and everyone and everything that I am associated with... they all belong to You. I also belong to You, and whoever I feel close to also belongs to You. I am content in the way You keep me."

## Principle 3: Attain blessings and share with others

The nature of the human mind is such that it does not feel gratitude for what it has. Feeling grateful is farfetched; it does not even notice or acknowledge what is received. However, it keeps lamenting about what is lacking. This sense of lack seems like a significant deficiency, leading to discontentment. If you want to remain content, feel grateful for your blessings, and share them with others as much as possible. It is a law of nature that what we share with others multiplies in our own lives. It is not just money that you can share; many other things can also be shared. You can support someone in their sorrow. If you have any specific talent or skill, you can share it with others. You can also share knowledge, happiness, joy, and information with others.

## Principle 4: Listen to the inner wise voice

Everyone has everything that they need. It is only our mind that compares whatever we have with others, leading to a sense of lack. We must stop listening to our mind and start listening to our inner wise voice—the voice of conscience. Our inner voice will show us the clear and correct picture as it is, without any comparison or bias, and will guide us to do the right things. Hence, connect with your conscience, listen to the inner wise voice, and avoid getting trapped in unnecessary feelings of discontentment.

## Principle 5: Believe in the law of karma

The law of karma states a very simple truth—our feelings, thoughts, speech, and actions come back to us in the form of karmic results. Therefore, never harbor discontentment and avoid saying things like, "Why did this happen to me when I have done nothing wrong?" or "I wish that had happened." If you want to change your future, first change your present thoughts, feelings, words, and actions and gracefully accept the karmic results of your previous actions. Those who have faith in the law of karma never choose to remain in discontentment; rather, they perform the right actions with contentment and enthusiasm.

## Principle 6: Work toward fulfilling the purpose of life on Earth

To remain content, we must know the fundamental purpose of our life on Earth. This is because until we know our true purpose, we adopt a different goal, borrowed from what we see around us. We assume the purpose is to earn more money and fame and accumulate more comforts and conveniences. We try to fulfill this purpose at the cost of our peace and contentment. At such times, we fail to realize what can actually lead to our progress.

We have not come to Earth to lead a life of comforts, but rather to develop divine virtues within us. They include love, bliss, peace, compassion, forgiveness, empathy, courage, patience, creativity, and contentment. When we strive to inculcate these divine virtues within us, worldly success comes as a bonus. However, in ignorance, in the pursuit of attaining worldly success, we neglect these virtues and tread the wrong path, leading to our downfall rather than progress.

Therefore, understand that life on Earth is like a school where we are given difficult circumstances and challenges, which serve as tests for us. It is by facing them gracefully that our virtues grow. For example, if someone does not behave properly with us, it is an opportunity for us to cultivate virtues like love, forgiveness, empathy, and patience. Therefore, our contentment should be associated with the nurturing of divine virtues, not with the acquisition of worldly pleasure and success.

---

> We can either live in the present, or think about life.
> Both cannot happen at the same time.
> Hence, stop thinking and start living.

---

### Principle 7: This is that what I need

In the sixth principle, we learned that, "The main purpose of our life on Earth is to cultivate divine virtues and attain spiritual growth." Keeping this in mind, we must learn to face challenges. If something is happening against your will or you feel something is missing, use the mantra, "This is that what I need." Also, understand that certain situations have occurred in your life as opportunities to cultivate some divine virtues within you.

Then face the situation with full awareness, understanding, and acceptance in such a way that it furthers the development of divine virtues within you. Perceive that situation with the attitude: This is that which I need.

These are some principles, which when integrated into your life, can help you lead a life of happiness and contentment.

### Points for contemplation

Reflect on the principles and mantras given in the chapter. Try to implement them in your life with a firm intent. Then observe how much more contentment has grown in your life.

### Case study

Suppose you attended a seminar where the importance of life principles was explained. "Life principles act as a guide for our lives. Understanding them helps us attain our goals. Through the medium of life principles, we can adopt good values, honesty, and a positive outlook, which makes our lives complete and contented. These principles help us face challenges, stay positive, and progress. This is why life principles are important as they guide us on the right path to live life in a better way."

Inspired by this, what principles will you choose to adopt in your life? Contemplate and write them down.

---

You can mail your opinion or feedback on this book to: books.feedback@tejgyan.org

# About Sirshree

Sirshree's spiritual quest, which began during his childhood, led him on a journey through various schools of philosophy and meditation practices. He studied a wide range of literature on mind science and spirituality. After a long period of deep contemplation on the truth of life, his quest culminated in attaining the ultimate truth.

Sirshree espouses, "All spiritual paths that lead to the truth begin differently but culminate at the same point – Understanding. This understanding is complete in itself. Listening to this understanding is enough to attain the Truth." Over the last two decades, he has dedicated his life to raise mass consciousness.

Sirshree has delivered more than 4000 discourses that throw light on this understanding. He has designed a system for wisdom, which makes it accessible to all. This system has inspired people from all walks of life to progress on their journey of the Truth. Thousands of seekers join in a virtual prayer for World Peace and Global Healing daily at 9:09 am and 9:09 pm.

# About Tej Gyan Foundation

Tej Gyan Foundation is a non-profit organization founded on the teachings of Sirshree. The Foundation disseminates Tejgyan – the wisdom that guides one from self-development to Self-realization, leading towards Self-stabilization.

The Foundation's system for imparting wisdom has been assessed by international quality auditors and accredited with the ISO 9001:2015 certification. This wisdom has been presented in a simple, systematic, and practically applicable form that makes it accessible to people from all walks of life, regardless of religion, caste, social strata, country, or belief system.

The Foundation has centers in more than 400 cities and towns across India and other countries. The mission of Tej Gyan Foundation is to create a highly evolved society by leading seekers from negative thoughts to positive thoughts and further, from positive thoughts to Happy thoughts. A 'Happy thought' is the auspicious thought of being free from all thoughts, leading to the state of supreme bliss beyond thoughts.

If you seek such wisdom that leads you beyond mere knowledge, dissolves all problems, frees you from all limiting beliefs, reveals the true nature of divinity, and establishes you in the ultimate truth, then it is time to discover Tejgyan; it is time to rise above the mundane knowledge of words and experience Tejgyan!

# The MahaAasmani Magic of Awakening Retreat

## Self-development to Self-realization towards Self-stabilization

Do you wish to experience unconditional happiness that is not dependent on any reason? Happiness that is permanent and only increases with time? Do you wish to experience love, peace, self-belief, harmony in relationships, prosperity, and true contentment? Do you wish to progress in all facets of your life, viz. physical, mental, social, financial, and spiritual?

If you seek answers to these questions and are thirsty for the ultimate truth, then you are welcome to participate in the MahaAasmani Magic of Awakening retreat organized by Tej Gyan Foundation. This is the Foundation's flagship retreat based on the teachings of Sirshree.

**The purpose of this retreat**

The purpose of this retreat is that every human being should:

- Discover the answer to "Who am I" and "Why am I?" through direct experience and be established in ultimate bliss.

- Learn the art of living in the present, free from the burden of the past and the anxiety of the future.

- Acquire practical tools to help quieten the chattering mind and dissolve problems.

- Discover missing links in the practices of Meditation (*Dhyana*), Action (*Karma*), Wisdom (*Gyana*), and Devotion (*Bhakti*).

# About Books by Sirshree

Sirshree's published work includes more than 150 book titles, some of which have been translated into more than 10 languages. His literature provides a profound reading on various topics of practical living and unravels the missing links in karma, wisdom, devotion, meditation, and consciousness.

His books have been published by leading publishing houses like Penguin, Hay House, Bloomsbury, Wisdom Tree, Jaico, etc. "The Source" book series, authored by Sirshree, has sold over 10 million copies. Various luminaries and celebrities like His Holiness the Dalai Lama, publishers Mr. Reid Tracy, Ms. Tami Simon and Yoga Master Dr. B. K. S. Iyengar have released Sirshree's books and lauded his work.

**The Source**
Attain Both, Inner Peace
and Worldly success

**Awaken the Power of Faith**
Discover the 7 Principles of the
Highest Power of the Universe

To order books authored by Sirshree, login to:
www.gethappythoughts.org
For further details, call: +91 9011013210

# SELECT BOOKS AUTHORED BY SIRSHREE

   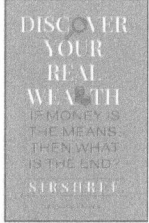

To order these and other books authored by Sirshree
Visit **www.gethappythoughts.org**

# Tej Gyan Foundation – Contact details

**Registered Office:**
Happy Thoughts Building, Vikrant Complex, Near Tapovan Mandir, Pimpri, Pune 411017, INDIA. Contact: +91 20-27411240, +91 20-27412576

**MaNaN Ashram:**
Survey No. 43, Sanas Nagar, Nandoshi Gaon, Kirkatwadi Phata, Off Sinhagad Road, Taluka Haveli, Pune district - 411024, INDIA. Contact: +91 992100 8060.

### WORLD PEACE PRAYER

*Divine Light of Love, Bliss, and Peace is Showering;*
*The Golden Light of Higher Consciousness is Rising;*
*All negativity on Earth is Dissolving;*
*Everyone is in Peace and Blissfully Shining;*
*O God, Gratitude for Everything!*

Members of Tej Gyan Foundation have been offering this impersonal mass prayer for many years. Those who are happy can offer this prayer. Those feeling low or suffering from illness can receive healing with this prayer.

If you are feeling troubled or sick, please sit to receive the healing effect of this prayer. Visualize that the divine white healing light is being showered on earth through the prayers of thousands and is also reaching you, bringing you peace and good health. You can dwell in this feeling for some time and then offer your gratitude to those offering the prayer.

**A Humble Appeal**

More than a million peace lovers pray for World Peace and Global Healing every morning and evening at 9:09. Also, a prayer (in Hindi) to elevate consciousness is webcast every day on YouTube at 3:30 pm and 9:00 pm IST. Please participate in this noble endeavor.

www.ingramcontent.com/pod-product-compliance
Lightning Source LLC
LaVergne TN
LVHW041847070526
838199LV00045BA/1483